SOCIAL ISSUES IN THE SEVENTIES
General Editor: J. N. Wolfe

---

2 Present and Future in Higher Education

SOCIAL ISSUES IN THE SEVENTIES

1 Meaning and Control
Edited by D. O. Edge and J. N. Wolfe

Present and Future
in Higher Education

Edited by

R. E. BELL

Lecturer, Faculty of Educational Studies, The Open University

and A. J. YOUNGSON

Vice Principal, University of Edinburgh, and Professor, Department of Economics, University of Edinburgh

TAVISTOCK PUBLICATIONS

First published in 1973
by Tavistock Publications Limited
11 New Fetter Lane, London EC 4
and printed in Great Britain
in 10/12 Times Roman
by Butler & Tanner Ltd, Frome and London

© 1973 Seminars Committee of the
Faculty of Social Sciences of the University of Edinburgh

I SBN 1 422 74200 7

Contributions to the Seminar on Higher Education
held at the University of Edinburgh in December 1970

Distributed in the USA by
HARPER & ROW PUBLISHERS, INC.
BARNES & NOBLE IMPORT DIVISION

Contributors

W. H. F. BARNES Professor, Department of Philosophy, Victoria University of Manchester

MAX BELOFF Professor of Government and Public Administration, Department of Social Studies, University of Oxford; now Principal-designate, The University College at Buckingham

R. E. BELL Lecturer, Department of Educational Sciences, University of Edinburgh; now Lecturer, Faculty of Educational Studies, The Open University

P. H. CALDERBANK Professor, Department of Chemical Engineering, School of Engineering Science, University of Edinburgh

The late T. L. COTTRELL Principal, University of Stirling

NIGEL GRANT Lecturer, Department of Educational Sciences; now Reader, Department of Educational Studies, University of Edinburgh

LIAM HUDSON Professor, Department of Educational Sciences; now Professor, Centre for Research in the Educational Sciences, University of Edinburgh

HUGH KEARNEY Professor of Modern History, Department of History, University of Edinburgh

JOHN LOWE Director, Department of Adult Education and Extra-mural Studies; now Director of Extra-mural Studies and Head of Department, Department of Educational Studies, University of Edinburgh

ALAN THOMPSON Senior Lecturer, Department of Economics, University of Edinburgh; now Professor of the Economics of Government, Heriot-Watt University, Edinburgh

v

JOHN VAIZEY Professor, Department of Economics, Brunel University

J. STEVEN WATSON Principal, University of St Andrews

J. N. WOLFE Professor, Department of Economics, University of Edinburgh

SIR HENRY WOOD Principal, Jordanhill College of Education, Glasgow; now retired

ROGER YOUNG Headmaster, George Watson's College, Edinburgh

Contents

Preface   *page* ix

HUGH KEARNEY
Universities and society in historical perspective   1

R. E. BELL
The growth of the modern university   13

NIGEL GRANT
Structure of higher education: some international comparisons   29

T. L. COTTRELL
Role of the new universities   47

P. H. CALDERBANK
The balance between engineering science and practical
experience   55

LIAM HUDSON
The psychological basis of subject-choice   63

ROGER YOUNG
Sixteen to twenty-one: the 'debatable area'   75

ALAN THOMPSON
Role of the junior college   85

SIR HENRY WOOD
Colleges of education in the seventies   101

JOHN LOWE
The other side of the binary system   115

J. STEVEN WATSON
Types of higher education: comprehensive, coordinated, or
classified   129

J. N. WOLFE
A postgraduate revolution?   139

MAX BELOFF
Universities and the enemies of excellence   151

W. H. F. BARNES
Finance and control of universities: basic principles   159

JOHN VAIZEY
Planning of higher education in the seventies   171

Subject Index   185

Name Index   191

Preface

The papers in this volume were all delivered in the University of Edinburgh during December 1970 at a seminar organized by the Seminars Committee of the Faculty of Social Sciences in the University.

In the field of higher education events have moved swiftly since then, and some of the material is now of historical rather than contemporary interest. For example, the paper by Sir Henry Wood could take no account of the publication of the James Committee's Report on teacher training and its aftermath. Even so, historical interest may well eventually prove to be considerable for the papers do catch a moment when all kinds of doubts about the state and future of higher education were beginning to be discussed not only by student radicals but, in a new and open way, by academics not normally cast in the role of revolutionary.

In particular, new doubts were being expressed about the continuation of the present relationship between the university and other sectors of the educational system. It was symptomatic that the most regular attenders at seminar sessions were not university staff but the head-teachers of the secondary schools of Edinburgh, officials of the Scottish teachers' unions, and the heads of those polytechnic-like institutions that, in Scotland, are called central institutions.

At the same time a considerable body of traditional opinion suggested that perhaps the easiest way to avoid demarcation disputes between university and school on the one hand, or between university and other forms of higher education on the other, lies in a withdrawal by the universities from some border areas which they share with other institutions into those areas of 'excellence' and academic elitism where they believe their true function lies, although the truly traditional nature of that function and its universality in industrial societies were questioned in other papers.

The seminar as a whole presents an interesting discussion of many of the principal dilemmas facing British higher education as it enters the 1970s. One of the seminar's most interesting features is that these dilemmas were almost universally seen as British dilemmas rather than as Scottish or English ones; and those who deplore, in the style of George Davie, the erosion of a separate Scottish academic tradition were quick to see that most of those taking part in the seminar, even those normally employed in Scotland, took their first degree at Oxford or Cambridge (the classic qualification for the educational anglicizer!). It remains to be seen whether the dominating factor in the decade now begun will be the old pragmatism of the Scottish universities which had no scruples about sharing their role from time to time with both the secondary school and the other institutions of learning in their cities, or the post-Newmanian idealism (backed by American and German examples) which has turned British universities during the past hundred years into centres of academic excellence. Some would suggest that what is now needed is a new range of institutions altogether. If this is so, then it would be as well if the issues raised by these papers were pondered carefully before decision-making went beyond recall.

R. E. BELL

Universities and society in historical perspective

HUGH KEARNEY

Can a historian make a contribution to the considerations discussed in this volume? Perhaps – by reminding its authors of the dimension of time. The problems that are to be discussed here, though distinctive, are not unique to the present moment. Debates about the function of universities, the balance of subjects, and the expansion of numbers have occurred many times. In due course, this conference will take its place as one that reveals some of the preoccupations and the assumptions of a particular society at a particular moment. In looking ahead it is impossible not to be influenced by the past, if only by reaction against it.

My theme is a discussion of stability and change in higher education over the past six centuries, a task that I will reduce to manageable proportions by confining my attention to a single case study – England. Here is a society, conveniently to hand, in which institutions of 'higher' education have existed since the thirteenth century. The assumptions made in it about the nature of higher education, the decisions taken and the changes that occurred over time are illuminating in themselves and offer the possibility of making comparisons with other societies.

For most of the period under discussion, England was essentially an aristocracy of landowners. The social assumptions on which it was governed and administered were those of the landed estate writ large. The king was the chief landowner and though due deference was paid to the crown, the monarchy was in effect an elective institution. There was of course a merchant class, but no sooner was a fortune made in the city than it was spent in acquiring an estate in the country. The tone of life was set by the aristocracy and until well after the Industrial Revolution the government of England was conducted by a cabinet in which landlords predominated. Even as late as the end of the nineteenth century, Gladstone thought of the England of 1990 as one in which the great landed estates would still be intact.

The assumption that an elite based upon birth and landed wealth was the most desirable form of society did not go unchallenged. It was called into question during the hey-day of the Puritan movement from the mid-sixteenth to the mid-seventeenth century. The Puritans believed that hierarchy in society should be based upon the principle of the godly elect, and Thomas Wood, a Puritan minister, had no qualms in the 1570s about calling the earl of Leicester to account for his ungodly actions. The godly minister spoke to the landed aristocrat as an equal. But the aristocracy survived the shocks of the Puritan revolution, and later political upheavals, to dominate the political and social life of the eighteenth century. The Industrial Revolution strengthened the economic basis of the landed estate, and it was not until the decline of English agriculture in the 1870s that aristocracy was seriously undermined. Even then it was not until the First World War that the final, or perhaps the penultimate, chapter was written.

Our main question is how far the universities were influenced by, or themselves influenced, this society of which they formed part. From the thirteenth century to the early sixteenth, the universities were professional schools catering for the needs of a sub-society, the church. From the universities came a steady and growing stream of theologians and canon lawyers, the educated elite of the sub-society. The church formed almost a separate culture, the values of which were in sharp contrast with those of the dominant military aristocracy. These twin elites in church and state each influenced the other. Respect for literacy spread among the laymen; the lay landlords often exercised local control over the church. A secular equivalent of the universities appeared in the Inns of Court. Abbots and bishops sat in the House of Lords next to their lay counterparts.

The balance of subjects taught within the universities was dictated by the presumed needs of the sub-society that they served. The arts faculty was a junior faculty staffed by aspiring young men and teaching disciplines considered to be relevant to the study of theology, or canon law. Among these so-called arts, logic held pride of place. But professional expertise did not exclude the advancement of learning, and some historians of ideas maintain that logic reached a stage of development in the fifteenth century that was not reached again until the twentieth. There are also grounds for thinking that the study of nature made far more headway during the middle ages than was once thought. Nevertheless these activities were not the major concern of the universities. Most of the students who came to them came to make a career in the church or to improve their status in society at a time when to be a 'clerk' carried legal privileges and the status of being literate at a time when literacy was the prerogative of the favoured few. The universities in short were the organs of an ecclesiastical elite, though this did not exclude some measure of social mobility.

During the early sixteenth century the first major change in English university history took place. In effect, the profession of canon law was abolished and with it much of the *raison d'être* of the university structure. The dissolution of the monasteries also removed an important section of the university community. It was possible that the universities themselves might have disappeared, to be succeeded by an expanded Inns of Court and by local seminaries catering for the diocesan clergy. Instead, Oxford and Cambridge received royal endowment of professorship and colleges on a grand scale. This was no doubt a decision made on intellectual grounds, but it was also, and perhaps most of all, part of a policy to secure religious, political, and social orthodoxy throughout the country.

Indeed, the reasons for these changes may be sought in part in the need to provide bulwarks of orthodoxy in a time of rapid religious and social change. The new regius professorships were royal nominees and the new royal colleges were visible reminders of the power and patronage of the state. In much of this the hand of Thomas Cromwell may be seen. But there were also sources of change within the universities associated with intellectual fashion and with the belief that the traditional disciplines were now outmoded. There were the makings of a generation gap here and of discontent based on social grievances of 'alienated intellectuals' within the clerical body. Finally, there was religious feeling and the demand for reform on religious grounds, which was associated with the movement for an educated laity at the upper social levels.

The net result of these changes was to set the social tone of the universities for the next three centuries. They now became institutions that catered for laymen as well as clerics. To go to these

institutions became a sign of status in either church or state. As Sir
Thomas Smith (1906) observed:

> For whosoever studies the laws of the realm, who studies at the
> universities, who professes liberal sciences and to be short who can
> live idly and without manual labour and will bear the port, charge
> and countenance of a gentleman, he should be called master . . .
> and taken for a gentleman.

At a time when the laws were beginning to penalize those who were
not 'gentlemen', the need for this status became increasingly obvious.
This is no doubt part of the explanation for the extraordinary rise
in student numbers during the late sixteenth century and the first
half of the seventeenth. There were also attractions in being a clergy-
man in a period of economic depression.

The balance of subjects within the university changed to some
extent over the period, but it bore the marks of the Renaissance and
the Reformation for a long time. Rhetoric, moral philosophy, and
history were part of the staple diet, all of them drawn from the
ancient classical authors. Part of the medieval curriculum survived
in the form of Aristotelian philosophy. Bacon criticized the universities for being too professional in their outlook and called for a
greater emphasis upon research into the secrets of nature. To some
extent his call was heeded, witness the foundation of the Oxford
Philosophical Society in the 1680s, but research within the universities bore the impress of its origins. It was religious in its inspiration
and often clerical. It also tended to be influenced, for good or ill, by
the ideal of the gentleman, Robert Boyle being the classical case.
Newton also in his scientific work was moved to some extent by
religious considerations.

For many critics, however, these institutions were too secular in
their outlook. The sectarian leader, Henry Barrow, writing in the
1590s wanted to abolish the universities and set up institutions in at
least 'every city in the land', where the tongues and other godly arts
should be taught (1966). During the Puritan revolution, the Digger
Gerard Winstanley, among others, denounced 'the universities [as]
the standing ponds of stinking waters'. It was complained that they
turned to Aristotle instead of the Bible:

> Out of his ethickes, economickes and politickes they fetch the
> order and government of their maners, private estate and common-
> wealth. He yet further instructed them of the soule and of the

worlde in lardge and speciale bookes of the heavens, of natural
and supernatural things of Nature, Fortune, the eternitie of the
world and perpetuitie of all creatures in their kind in specie . . .

There was also a social dimension to these criticisms which came
from the feeling that the universities monopolized learning in the
interests of the established social order. Clergy were denounced
along with the lawyers, and even physicians, as enemies of the
liberty of the commonwealth. Hence the attempt that was made to
abolish the universities by the Barebones Parliament in 1653 at the
height of the Puritan revolution. But the universities, like the aristocracy, survived the crisis. Parson and squire grew closer together than
they had been before. What this might mean at the level of village
life is described satirically by Joseph Arch, the founder of the
agricultural labourers' union (as quoted in Warwick 1898):

First, up walked the squire to the communion rails; the farmers
went up next; then up went the tradesmen, the shopkeepers, the
wheelwright and the blacksmith; and then, the very last of all,
went the poor agricultural labourers in their smock frocks. They
walked up by themselves; nobody else knelt with them; it was as
if they were unclean . . .

With the impact of the Industrial Revolution from the early
nineteenth century and the associated factors of urbanization,
political change, and the shift in the balance of social power from
countryside to town, it was inevitable that the nature of higher
education should become the centre of fierce debate. To the supporters of utilitarianism, Oxford and Cambridge seemed to provide
an education that was increasingly irrelevant to the needs of the day.
Their pressures led in 1828 to the foundation of University College,
London, which in its secular, practical emphasis was poles apart
from the current universities. It seemed to many that this was the
pattern of the future, a higher education directed towards Benthamite
utility and expertise. The foundation of University College was
followed eventually (in 1851) at Manchester with the establishment
of Owens College. For both colleges, the influence of the Dissenting
Academies of the eighteenth century was important. In Manchester,
Arthur Thomas Barnes, Minister of Cross Street Chapel, imagined

a system of education for a commercial man which shall contain all the parts of science proper for him to know, as much as

possible in practical form and which amidst all the other objects
of study shall keep this point continually in view . . . (Charlton
1951).

The influence of a Scottish university model was also important
by reason of its emphasis upon relatively cheap, non-residential,
higher education. In fact, many of the early professors at University
College, London, were Scots. Thomas Jefferson's new University of
Virginia (opened 1825) was also a source of inspiration. For all the
emphasis on cheapness, however, University College, London, was
a middle-class venture. Law and medicine occupied a prominent
place in the curriculum, and Thomas Campbell saw as its aim to serve
the 'middling rich', the 'small comfortable trading fortunes'. It was
to be an institution adapted to the circumstances of all that class of
society 'whose monies extend from £400 or £500 a year, to nearly as
many thousands'.

The exposition of an alternative point of view found classical form
in Newman's *The Idea of a University* (1853). For Newman, liberal
education was an end in itself, but his lectures, delivered in the
obscurity of a Dublin Hall to an audience of Irish bishops, did not
have the effect that is often attributed to them. The decisive voice in
answering the challenge to the ancient universities was that of
Benjamin Jowett, fellow of Balliol and, from 1870, Master of the
College. Oxford and Cambridge were to take up the challenge of
educating the new urbanized elite. Jowett's proudest achievement
was the creation of a new school of 'Literae Humaniores' at Oxford,
which along with three other honours schools of law, modern history,
and natural science formed the basis of changes in the curriculum.
Jowett put his trust in classics, history, and philosophy, nevertheless
his reforms were based upon a disguised utilitarianism or rather the
need to provide the university with a social function in which service
to the state would replace service to the church. He is quoted in
Abbott and Campbell (1897):

> There is nothing I less wish than to see Oxford turned into a
> German or a London University. On the other hand, is it at all
> probable that we shall be allowed to remain as we are for twenty
> years longer, the one solitary, exclusive, unnational Corporation –
> our enormous wealth *without any manifest utilitarian purpose*; a
> place, the studies of which belong to the past, and unfortunately
> seem to have no power of incorporating new branches of

knowledge; so exclusive, that it is scarcely capable of opening to the wants of the Church itself?

These changes were not entirely divorced from religious considerations. Jowett and his allies within Oxford saw themselves as part of a modernizing movement within the Church of England that would save it from the dangers of the Oxford Movement. The reforms that he helped to introduce broke the monopoly of the clergy in the colleges, allowed for the admission of dissenters, and eventually did away with the obligation upon celibacy. The four new schools that were introduced now offered an alternative to theology. Jowett hoped that 'improved scholarships would provide the means for many more persons of the middling class to find their way through the university into professions'.

Perhaps the most remarkable change that occurred at Oxford and Cambridge was the way in which the two universities became a training ground for the new breed of civil servants that came into existence as a result of the Northcote–Trevelyan report (1853). Increasingly from the 1860s and 1870s onwards, the universities were the source of a new governing elite in England and in her Indian Empire. Macaulay (as quoted in Trevelyan 1876) was moved to eloquence at the prospect of an empire ruled by trained minds:

It is said, I know, that examinations in Latin, in Greek, and in Mathematics are not tests of what men will prove to be in life. I am perfectly aware that they are not infallible tests; but that they are tests I confidently maintain. Look at every walk of life, at this House, at the other House, at the Bar, at the Bench, at the Church, and see whether it be not true that those who attain high distinction in the World were generally men who were distinguished in their academic career. Whether the English system of education be good or bad is not now the question. Perhaps I may think that too much time is given to the ancient languages and to the abstract sciences, which it is, in any age or country, the fashion to teach, the persons who become the greatest proficients in those languages and those sciences will generally be the flower of the youth; the most acute, the most industrious, the most ambitious of honourable distinctions. If the Ptolemaic system were taught at Cambridge instead of the Newtonian, the senior wrangler would, nevertheless, be in general a superior man to the wooden spoon . . . If alchymy were taught, the young man who showed most activity in the pursuit of the philosopher's stone would generally turn out a superior man.

Sir Charles Trevelyan, the reformer of the civil service, put the vision into practice. As he saw it (in Hanham 1969; see also Parris 1969): 'the effect of a system will be to secure for the public offices the best portion of the best educated of our youth'. And he continued:

> Who are so successful in carrying off the prizes at competing scholarships, fellowships, &c. as the most expensively educated young men? Almost invariably, the sons of gentlemen, or those who by force of cultivation, good training and good society have acquired the feelings and habits of gentlemen. The tendency of the measure, will I am confident, be decidedly aristocratic, but it will be so in a good sense by securing for the public service those who are, in a true sense, 'the best'. At present a mixed multitude is sent up, a large proportion of whom, owing to the operation of political and personal patronage, are of an inferior rank of society . . . and they are, in general, the least eligible of their respective ranks . . . All this will be remedied by the proposed arrangement . . .

Balliol under Jowett was at the centre of these developments. It was no accident that Plato's *Republic* with its vision of an elite of Guardians should become a set book for the new school of Greats. A pupil remarked of Jowett, 'He was a Platonist all over and from Plato I never could extract more than one graspable idea and that was the education of his ideal governors'. In fact, Jowett envisaged a limit of 3,000 students for Oxford.

While England moved towards competitive examinations for her civil service, administrative reforms were being criticized in the United States, on the ground that they would lead to the creation of an aristocracy. Frederick Woodbridge made the following remarks[1] in the House of Representatives in 1867 on Jencke's bill for administrative reform:

> But, sir, there are other objections to the bill. One is that it is anti-democratic. My friend from Rhode Island has said, and it is undoubtedly true, that Belgium and Prussia and France and England have a similar system of appointing officers to the civil service. But where is the analogy between England and this country? That, sir, is a country of aristocracy, a country of classes, where as

a rule a man cannot rise unless he is born to position. In England the coal-heaver of today is a coal-heaver on the day of his death. Here the avenues to position, to power, to wealth, are open to all, and they ought not by any legislation of ours to be closed. . . . The race is to all men. The avenues are all open; and I think it would be dangerous for us to close these avenues to the many and provide a royal road for a fortunate or favoured few. . . .

Viewpoints resembling Woodbridge's did not go unexpressed in England. Such men as Thomas Henry Huxley, scientist and popularizer, hoped for social mobility in education, but his ideas did not make much headway, perhaps because of his views on religion, perhaps also because no appropriate educational ladder leading from school to university existed for most of the population.

There was yet another ideal for higher education, that of culture for its own sake, eloquently expounded by Arnold and Mark Pattison among others. In a speech at Liverpool in 1876 Mark Pattison (quoted in Sparrow) said:

It is no part of the proper business of a university to be a professional school. Universities are not to fit men for some special mode of gaining a livelihood; their object is not to teach law or divinity, banking or engineering, but to cultivate the mind and form the intelligence.

Earlier Matthew Arnold had said that the prime aim of education was 'to enable a man to know himself and the world'.

Of these three ideals of higher education the dominant was that aiming to educate a governing elite, but the other two ideals were also represented among the dons of Oxford and Cambridge. Culture and vocationalism coexisted but at the end of the century the balance of subjects within Oxford and Cambridge was weighted in favour of disciplines thought to be appropriate for the education for leadership at home and abroad. Classics, philosophy, and history were particularly in evidence. Skills associated with commerce were kept at arm's length, but training associated with the 'liberal' professions of law and medicine was acceptable. Natural science was the odd man out, and even at Cambridge it was unusual for a scientist to be made a fellow of his college.

Though the two ancient universities continued to dominate the academic scene, a system of urban colleges came into existence, some of them based upon existing local institutions. In their curriculum, subjects with a vocational character predominated, to provide training for local professional classes. Their prestige and income at this time were low and their students few. The total number of fulltime day students taking a degree at universities and colleges outside Oxford and Cambridge amounted to less than 5,000 in 1912–13. The total reached 7,600 when diploma and graduate students were included and reached 13,800 only when parttime students of all kinds were included. Of the seventeen universities and colleges receiving a grant from the exchequer, less than half had over 500 fulltime students, and only one had over 1,000. Moreover, at this date, numbers were falling, a fact that was commented upon in the Board of Education report (1912–13). The passage is worth quoting for the light it throws upon what officialdom considered to be the point of going to university:

It would appear that the rate of increase in the number of full-time students has been diminishing for some years past. The position is not satisfactory from the wider national standpoint. There is little doubt that the commercial prosperity of the country during recent years has had a good deal to do with this diminution in the number of students who are seeking a University education. Only a minority of these schools send students to the Universities unless they happen to be placed in or very near to the University towns. It is not suggested that it would benefit all boys to go to a University without regard to their means or their ability and without a careful selection of their course of study, but there are grounds for thinking that the demand for healthy and able young men with a University training is beginning to outrun the supply. The openings for administrators of various kinds and for teachers in the Indian Empire and in the Crown Colonies are increasing in number, while suitable candidates are not. Nor is the demand confined to service abroad. The Royal Commissioners on the Civil Service are evidently of opinion that the newer Universities are not contributing a due proportion of candidates for the Home Services. 'We should be glad', they say, 'to see the Scottish, the Irish, and the young English' and Welsh Universities assert more vigorously their claim to 'share in Civil Service Appointments'. That they have not done so in the past is in part due, no doubt, to the character of the examination, but it is largely explained by the younger age at which their students – in itself evidence of a hurried education – and partly by the diversion of some of the brightest minds in the schools to the practical world of business before the secondary stage of their education is complete. It is doubtful whether even the commerce of the country will benefit in the long run by this impatience; it is certain that the national and imperial services lose the variety of training and upbringing which is to be desired in their recruits.

The editors of this report, one of whom was the permanent secretary, had no doubt that the object of university education was to supply administrators and teachers for the Indian Empire and the Crown Colonies. The provincial universities clearly did not fit into this scheme of things. In a more ambiguous world than Oxford or Cambridge they had to compete with the world of commerce for their supply of students.

Thus the establishment of the provincial universities was not in itself a challenge to the supremacy of Oxford and Cambridge which remained the only centres for the higher education of the English elite until the outbreak of the First World War. The impact of the war can scarcely be overrated and it is not too much to say that it marked the end of the aristocratic tradition in England. Trench warfare in France took a heavy toll among members of the governing elite, and in the postwar period the landed estate and the values it stood for gave way to those of the office and the factory. This removed one of the main social bases of the elitist tradition. Nevertheless much seemed to go on as before. The Empire survived the storm and in the eyes of its critics continued to provide a gigantic system of outdoor relief for the graduates of Oxford and Cambridge. The two universities continued to educate an elite and the nineteenth century curriculum remained, orientated towards this end. Some new disciplines were introduced, for example, Modern Greats at Oxford, which as the name implies was intended to be an up-to-date version of Jowett's concepts.

Perhaps this survey has been concentrated too much upon social influences and not enough upon what may be termed the self-generating factors in education. But these, it may be suggested, are more a phenomenon of the contemporary period, especially of the decades following the 1944 Education Act. I am content to end my account at the beginning of the Second World War, when the *ancien régime* was drawing to an end and the 'educational revolution' about to begin. Whether the changes are an unmixed blessing is a question that may safely be left to discussion, but it seems likely that the new will be as open to criticism as the old.

NOTE

[1] See Hoogenboom 1964. I owe this reference to my colleague K. Hampson.

REFERENCES

ABBOTT, E. and CAMPBELL, L. 1897. *Life and Letters of Benjamin Jowett.* London.

BARROW, H. 1966. *The Writings of Henry Barrow 1590–91.* London: Allen & Unwin.

Board of Education. *Reports from Universities receiving Grants 1912–13,* I: xi.

CHARLTON, H. B. 1951. *Portrait of a University.* Manchester: Manchester University Press.

WARWICK, COUNTESS OF (ed.). 1898. *Joseph Arch: The Story of his Life.* London.

HANHAM, H. J. (ed.). 1969. *The Nineteenth-century Constitution.* Cambridge: Cambridge University Press.

HOOGENBOOM, A. 1964. *Spoilsmen and Reformers.* New York: Rand.

PARRIS, H. 1969. *Constitutional bureaucracy.* London: Kelley.

SMITH, SIR THOMAS. 1906. L. Alston (ed.), In *De republica anglorum.* Cambridge: Cambridge University Press.

SPARROW, J. 1967. *Mark Pattison and the Idea of a University.* Cambridge: Cambridge University Press.

TREVELYAN, G. O. 1961. *Life and Letters of Lord Macaulay.* London: Oxford University Press.

NEWMAN, JOHN H. 1971. *The Idea of a University.* London: Holt, Rinehart & Winston.

The growth of the modern university

R. E. BELL

Since the foundation of the University Grants Committee and even more since the general rise in university entrance requirements during the 1950s, there has been a growing tendency to regard all British universities as equal, at least in scope and function. Underlying the claims of the *Black Papers*, and, indeed, underlying the Robbins Report itself, is not only an assumption of common aims and standards that would have astonished academics even in the 1940s, but also an even clearer assumption that the 'traditional' role and status of the university is self-evident, endorsed by decades, if not centuries, of usage and experience. The purpose of this paper is to suggest that, in Britain at any rate, such assumptions are historically invalid, and can be dangerously misleading when reference to 'traditional role' becomes an emotive ingredient in any discussion of the future pattern of the higher education system as a whole.

Until the 1960s both the British academic and the British layman were clearly aware that 'university' was no unitary concept. Categorization of institutions was usually crude, as in the meaningless dichotomy of 'Oxbridge' and 'Red Brick' which lumped St Andrews with Hull and LSE with Aberystwyth, and ignored the many characteristics that Oxford and Cambridge shared with other institutions (for example, with Durham as a residential collegiate university, with Manchester as a centre of elitist research, and with London as part of a metropolitan culture). Equally meaningless, since it ignored functions, was the common division into ancient and modern, with Dublin and Edinburgh uneasily occupying some chronological middle-ground as models of the 'civic' university (an equally misleading phrase).

Even the many categorizations based on slightly subtler historical analyses, such as the one that posed models of 'Paris' and 'Bologna', depended on the naïve assumption that universities remain frozen in polarized administrative states for long periods of time. It depended also on the even more naïve assumption that British universities have ever self-consciously accepted such clear-cut foreign models without considerable local modification. Yet the old (Parisian?) picture of the dedicated scholar (research worker?) kindly allowing a brood of young men to sit at his feet in earnest apprenticeship is still sufficiently flattering to academic self-esteem for it to have lost none of its potency. However, the alternative (Bolognese?) model, believed (probably falsely) to be perpetuated in the Scottish rectorial system, of a band of students employing a servile professor to teach them at their whim seems now to have lost its earlier appeal.

Far less crude was the categorization offered by the Principal of Edinburgh at the opening of the session of 1870–71 when he classified British universities as the 'collegiate' (in the style of Oxford, Cambridge, and Durham) allowing students privileged entry into a 'traditional' community of scholars; the 'professorial' (the Scottish universities and the new English colleges at Manchester and London which had been modelled upon them); and the 'non-teaching' university, the university purely as an examination board (of which the University of London was then the prime example, but the idea of which underlay both the future Royal University of Ireland and the Victoria University in Lancashire and Yorkshire). Yet, even in 1870, such a threefold categorization was becoming far from satisfactory. Trinity College, Dublin, had characteristics both of 'collegiate' Cambridge and of 'professorial' Edinburgh. Oxford and Cambridge themselves were already beginning to emphasize once more the importance of the university, as opposed to the college, as a major teaching agency with the newly active professors attracting mass audiences in Scottish style. It is useful also to remember that even the notion of 'university as examination board' had had its origins in Oxford (where the state used it to break the colleges' strangle-hold on teaching), and that Gladstone, for largely Oxonian reasons, was anxious to impose on the Scottish universities (or 'colleges' as Edinburgh still liked to call them) a federal structure which in his opinion could alone ensure adequate examination standards.

However, all such twentieth- and later nineteenth-century categorizations make the same assumption that, whatever their individual academic or social standing, 'universities' form a recognizable group quite separate from all other forms of educational institution, and, perhaps too glibly, we now readily assume that Victorian notions of demarcation and of internal functioning must therefore correspond very largely to our own. In fact, however, the legal and 'traditional' bases of the universities' present exclusive functions do not always stand up well to close examination. Certainly the apparently timeless trappings of university life are, even now, far from being protected legally. Universities have, for example, no exclusive rights to the use of the term 'professor', despite the charisma that has protected its recent use in British circles. It is, for example, used widely in Catholic secondary schools as well as in bodies such as the Royal Academy. The university cannot even challenge the use of its academic dress by outside bodies, as Aberdeen discovered when they attempted to prevent the local art college from stealing their MA hood. Even the right to grant degrees, now commonly seen as the exclusive mark of the true university, need not depend on any charter and is in any case available to many other chartered bodies such as the professional colleges or the Educational Institute of Scotland, while the Council for National Academic Awards (not to mention the Archbishop of Canterbury) actually use the university nomenclature when doing so. Perhaps, however, the term least protected until usage made it so in recent times, is the word 'university' itself. Here, as in North America it was for long interchangeable with 'college' and with 'school' as a description of institutions ranging from dancing academies through Glasgow's Andersonian University (which began much of modern technological education) to those institutions which have now, finally, claimed an exclusive right to it.

Thus, when in the 1820s Brougham and his supporters first planned their establishment in Gower Street called the 'University of London' (later University College), they did not necessarily have in mind, as later general historians have assumed, a middle-class equivalent of Oxford. Such equivalents, often educationally superior, were already readily available in the Dissenting Academies, which were largely unhampered by their inability to award degrees. The 'University of London' offered a metropolitan centre of educational activity, free from religious tests. The wishes and nature of its customers alone were eventually to decide its place in a spectrum in which the educational status (as opposed to the social status) even of Oxford and Cambridge remained far from clear. Brougham himself declared that he saw his new 'University' as providing for London what the Royal High School provided for Edinburgh (Hale Bellott 1929); at no stage did he appear to see it as a degree-granting body until its Anglican rivals, King's and Durham, began to move in that direction. When a 'true', i.e. a degree-granting, University of London was finally established in 1836, it took the form of a governing board with the staff of the various teaching colleges – of which Brougham's was but one – having little or no say in its examinations until as late as 1900.

Thus, before 1850 the notion of a university was, in British terms, clearly a vague one and to many fellows of Cambridge colleges the 'university' as such often represented the 'enemy' threatening his privileges throughout the period of reform.

Moreover, throughout the nineteenth century, the 'true' functions and style of what universities there were in Britain tended to be equally disputed even among academics themselves. Newman's *Idea of a University* written in the 1850s has come to be regarded (largely by those who have not read it carefully) as a statement of 'traditional' belief concerning the nature of the university. Yet, despite its defence of 'liberal' values, it is far from presenting a picture of any British university that existed at that time or of any university likely to be present in the minds of our twentieth-century defenders of academic standards. It then represented an almost totally idiosyncratic position. Newman believed, for example, in the notion of the university as a living community of like-minded scholars of assorted ages at a time when almost all the Scottish universities and even many Oxford and Cambridge dons (Thomas Arnold among them) saw the drawing of young men out of the religious safeguards of the home into an artificial community as a danger to morality and, at best, a necessary evil.

Indeed, except in a few colleges such as Newman's own, the college tutor of the early nineteenth century was at best a schoolmaster and at worst a policeman, the proctor with his bulldogs, with little about him of that housemasterly or even scholarly figure which he later became. Not until well after 1900 did Glasgow or Edinburgh encourage students' residences and Patrick Geddes's late nineteenth-century establishment in Ramsey Garden, Edinburgh, was both disapproved of and opposed as a betrayal of Scottish tradition.

Newman also believed in a breadth of curriculum totally unacceptable to the vested interests and superstitions of contemporary academics, even in Scotland. He was opposed to 'practical' professional studies, perhaps the one genuinely traditional element in the university of his day and a major spur to nineteenth-century reform. Above all he was totally opposed to the pursuit of scientific research within the university itself and to the all too common modern notion of a don so continually and rightly at the frontiers of knowledge that to return to teach the undergraduate becomes an act of grace and favour. He saw his don as being principally paid to teach and the university as merely one of the many academically elitist teaching institutions in the country. Clearly in terms of 1970 this is neither the traditional nor the convenient view for those who prefer the (Parisian?) myth of the charismatic research-worker gathering his eager but ignorant students around him.

Newman's lectures were originally delivered in connection with the founding of an abortive Catholic university in Dublin, and this in itself reminds us that, until the late nineteenth century, the idea of the university as the imposer of a single version of religious belief did not come strangely to the Oxford or Cambridge don. At least until the 1850s he assumed his right to regulate not merely the religious but also, on occasions, the political activities of those who came into his charge. The Scottish universities' persistent refusal to accept such a role, or indeed any role *in loco parentis*, provided perhaps the greatest single contrast between English and Scottish institutions. Certainly general university freedom of belief and preaching is a comparatively recent innovation so far as England is concerned. Freedom of institutional arrangements there may have been; freedom of speech was another matter.

In addition, Newman envisaged his potential students as coming from a much younger age-group than today and, in many instances, it is clear that throughout the nineteenth century the university continued to provide, for those who wished, a general education now clearly delegated to the secondary school. Both at Edinburgh (as late as 1881)[1] and in the London colleges (in mid-century) local schools were often in open competition with the universities themselves for students of the same age and academic standard. At King's College, London, the pupils of its own school (ostensibly preparatory) were often said to be both older and more ably taught than in the 'higher' institution (Hearnshaw 1929, 192). Both

Oxford and Cambridge consciously negotiated with the public schools for the gradual handing over to the latter of the generalist education previously the concern of undergraduate courses. The distinction between the natures of secondary and tertiary education was – and is – far from traditionally fixed. Thomas Arnold for example, writing to the original senate of London University, saw its BA as potentially the equivalent of sixth-form work at Rugby, and where academic entrance requirements to tertiary education existed they were (until after 1900) normally of an extremely undemanding kind. In Scotland, until the 1890s, the very idea of their introduction was seen as a national betrayal. It is true that Marischal College in Aberdeen had for long had such entrance requirements but, on merging with King's College, Aberdeen, in 1860 the latter (as the senior institution) insisted on their being abandoned, specifically in the name of 'tradition'.[2]

Clearly there is little of current academic elitism in this picture. Even after the changes of the 1850s, the Scottish universities continued to be generally regarded in England (along with the new English colleges) as essentially secondary institutions of the German kind. An early volume of the journal *Mind* (2, 74ff) had to allow Scottish academics to defend themselves against such charges. Scottish and Irish honours graduates, however distinguished, continued for many decades to pass on not to postgraduate study at Oxford and Cambridge, but to the elitist undergraduate study that was seen as starting where their wide, but shallow, 'general' education had left off. Statistically too, the Scottish universities do not suggest either academic or social elitism.

Indeed, there is a case for examining whether such institutions in Scotland and England were, in fact, performing similar social or academic functions, and now to class them together may be misleading and unfair to both. The number of matriculated male students in Edinburgh in 1889 (almost all of them undergraduates) was 3,576, and while numbers dropped by a thousand ten years later as a result of stricter entrance requirements male undergraduate numbers did not reach such a peak again until they were exceeded in 1962. Even as late as 1920 when the populations of England and Scotland were in the ratio of 9 to 1, the university populations were 3 to 1.

The Scottish universities were to a much greater extent dominated by a wide range of professions (particularly medicine and school-teaching) than were Oxford and Cambridge which came, once the church had been largely set aside, to be dominated by the academic profession itself. Indeed, the spread of the Oxford and Cambridge academic career structure so as to include Scotland and the other English institutions was in itself to prove a cause of tension.

George Davie (1961) has rightly made much of the introduction of English-style honours degrees to Scotland after 1858. This need not, of course, have the anti-nationalist significance that he gives it. It may well be seen as yet another manifestation of greater social complexity in an expanding economy. Nevertheless, at Glasgow, for example, though there were always, between 1889 and 1900, some two thousand matriculated students, the number graduating with honours in any one year never rose above thirty-eight, and in one year (1892–93) it fell as low as four. Indeed, throughout the nineteenth century, a major problem in Scotland and in Ireland was how to persuade a student to attend whole courses and to graduate at all. The style and the level of attendance and aspiration for the majority of students had far more in common with modern further education colleges than with the modern university. The holding of DP certificates (guaranteeing that the work of a class had been 'duly performed') was a sufficient meal ticket for most professional situations, and elitist educational changes such as the introduction of English-style tutorials at undergraduate level could, as Jennie Lee (1963) has described, cause actual strikes among students, avid for lecture notes, as late as 1924. The colleges at London and Manchester, modelled on Scotland, faced similar problems of low aspiration and expectation.

George Davie has, of course, also rightly reminded us that there were earlier periods of great academic glory in Scotland just as, even in the darkest periods of the eighteenth century, there were distinguished research workers, and teachers among Cambridge dons. Nevertheless, such famous figures remain almost certainly the statistical exception, and one must not ignore the fact that far more distinguished researchers and teachers made their impact outside the university altogether. It remains a challenging fact that the period from 1700 to 1850, one of the greatest periods of British intellectual, industrial, and scientific development, happened also to be the period when the universities were at their lowest academic ebb. The portraits of distinguished men, the magnificent old libraries, and the current activities of particular institutions must not blind us to the fact that the majority of their inhabitants, during a considerable period of their existence, were in no sense part of any academic elite, and that for most of their lives, our present 'ancient' universities were, even by the standards of their own day, performing functions now performed by secondary schools or colleges of further education, while their current functions of research and technical advising were largely being performed by other bodies and institutions altogether.

This was far less true of Germany and even of the United States, and perhaps when the British academic speaks of his 'tradition' it is, not without reason, a European or an Anglo-Saxon rather than a British tradition that he has in mind. The present elitist function of the British university is a late nineteenth-century innovation based upon imported models, which prompted individuals, and eventually the state, to force what were highly resistant, socially elitist institutions into largely new patterns of behaviour.

It is remarkable, therefore, how little attention social scientists have paid to this sudden nineteenth-century change.[3] Clearly there is much to interest even the anthropologist in the way in which largely moribund ceremonial and examination structures suddenly achieved immense significance for those men of high intelligence who for decades had either satirized or ignored them completely. A structuralist investigation of the sudden revival of academic dress in Scotland could clearly illuminate other aspects of Victorian middle-class behaviour, such as the codification of games, again a development in a wholly academic context. It might also explain our continued reluctance to regularize a degree system that remains as chaotic as it was a hundred years ago.

However, perhaps even more fruitful scientific investigation would involve an approach to the growth of the modern university not in terms of intellectual activity (this has far too often been attempted in isolation from other factors) but in terms of the university's market economy and all that the economist and sociologist could say about it. For there is no superstition more misleading or more clearly nonsensical than the belief that universities were once interested in purely academic matters and only in recent decades have begun to be concerned obsessively with money.

It is, of course, true that before the abolition of life-fellowships dons in England never needed to worry about where the next meal was coming from, but their lives were still considerably dominated by matters of career, status, and patronage. The development of the Cambridge curriculum beyond the basic subjects of elementary classics and high level maths posed a considerable economic threat to personal and college earnings. Thus, all the triposes began as postgraduate courses, apparently so as not to threaten the posts and incomes of practising teachers. When any tripos was finally established, because much of the special advanced coaching was given by non-university teachers, it could be taken only as a second postgraduate qualification after the maths tripos for which official college teaching existed (Winstanley 1935). Hence the fanatical opposition to parliament's later removal of many financial securities in the interests of widening the curriculum. Ostensibly, of course, the objections made were academic, though when Cambridge men taught elsewhere – at Durham or at the Anglican King's College – their objections to such a widened curriculum quickly melted away. Reform, it is true, began inside Oxford and Cambridge but, until state intervention, the reformers remained a small and ineffectual minority, able to make little headway against vested interests and prejudice.

For much of the nineteenth century Oxford and Cambridge were dominated by the needs of a career structure that embraced not merely the colleges but the whole Church of England and the public schools. It was even possible to combine a headmastership with benefices or university chairs, as Thomas Arnold did. Teaching in socially elitist schools was never seen as being at a lower academic level. Movement from one of these sectors to another (for example, from a headmastership to a colonial bishopric) was extremely simple, and the whole structure carefully balanced. Clearly questions of conscience did not arise as issues except within extremely circumscribed (and purely Anglican) limits. Genuinely scholarly activity beyond the apprentice period, though it was not actually discouraged, produced little or no dividends. In mid-century, the state, apparently awakened to the threat of growing competition from countries with more sophisticated systems of higher education and to the demands of the Prince Consort[4] and the reforming dons themselves, proceeded to dismantle this whole edifice.

For the remainder of the century, government gave administrative and financial encouragement both to the more diversified lines of academic activity already being followed in Scotland, London, and Manchester, and to the provision of professional courses, especially in medicine. It also encouraged the drawing of the honours examinations into Oxford and Cambridge undergraduate courses, as a reformed secondary sector took over the university's earlier and more generalized educative functions. This latter process was, of course, also begun (but only half concluded) in the case of Scotland whose professors, financially more strained, still demanded every student they could get. Hence the present Scottish university curriculum with its un-English mixture of honours (specialist) and ordinary (generalist) education. University teachers, having been divested by government intervention (and the conscientious acts of some of their own members) of their earlier prestigeful, comfortable but academically non-elitist roles, began to turn to new roles which ensured for them a prestigeful position in the newly developing spectrum of higher education. The two ancient English universities defined this new role, in Jowett's Platonic terms, as the producer of leaders (political, scientific, and professional), and in order to facilitate the adoption of this role they made it easier for – though as yet they did not compel – their undergraduates to reach, more rapidly, academic levels of a clear distinction hitherto reserved for postgraduate students only. The Scottish universities, in a less rewarding economy, had lowlier aims – to provide courses of a high standard for entry to the professions (especially medicine and teaching) and within these limits to follow the fashionable English to the greatest extent possible. Clearly those Scots seeking political leadership had still to go south – if necessary, as postgraduate undergraduates!

The Scottish academics' desire to emulate the English is not only reflected in their growing tendency to recruit English 'beginners' as professors (thus drawing the Scottish universities into the more prestigeful English career structure), but also in the great respect shown by their academic selection committees to Oxford and Cambridge distinctions. It is shown also in the desire of both Edinburgh and St Andrews to play up their 'medieval' picturesqueness as a suitable setting for Oxford-style academic activity. (Glasgow, alas, which in Defoe's time had been said to be even more beautiful than either of the others had, by 1850, lost that particular academic or, possibly more truthfully, economic asset.) This anglicizing tendency was reflected even more in the Scottish universities' eventual attempts to cater especially for the products of the new, cheaper middle-class secondary schools (for example, in Edinburgh, Heriot's, Watson's and similar schools) which, after 1870, suddenly mushroomed in the major cities. The old 'open' procedure of going straight from village school to university became less and less possible.

The reform of the older establishments in England exposed the economics of their newer rivals; it is amusing to see how readily Durham, overtly founded to protect the dean and chapter's finances from government attack (Whiting 1932), quickly lowered its academic requirements in order to beat off its economic rivals. It began to offer colleges at all income levels (with consciously differing social tones) and was even willing to lop a year off its BA course in the interests of attracting custom. The London colleges tried a whole range of commercial experiments from offering military science at the time of the Crimea to preparing old Etonians for Oxford (Hearnshaw 1929, 181–4). Meanwhile, in Scotland, the economically more exposed Aberdeen and St Andrews, with their comparatively small numbers, fruitlessly tried to embrace, in the one case, the socially and academically suspect activity of training schoolteachers and, in the other, the unsuccessful Durham game of offering the social and medieval graces of Oxford without the latter's new-found academic rigour or its metropolitan prestige.

In general, the new elitism was slower off the ground in Scotland, partly because of the 'open' national tradition and, even more, because the institutions were poorly endowed and needed every reasonable student they could get. Thus, although the professors eventually gave up their practice of competing with schoolmasters in their teaching of 'pre-graduating' preparatory classes, and moved closer to a more academically respectable fixed salary situation so that their income did not rise and fall merely according to the number of students whom they could attract (rather in the style recently advocated by the Prices and Incomes Board), they were nevertheless clearly unwilling to abolish the ordinary arts classes which gave the university its basic income. The Scottish universities literally could not afford until much later to ignore the wishes of the professional associations or the Chambers of Commerce in the way that Oxford and Cambridge had earlier ignored the (in English early nineteenth-century terms) non-elitist professions of medicine and engineering.[5] Even so, despite the fact that the Scottish secondary teachers had achieved growing academic prestige, the internal vested interests of the university could still prevent full Scottish acceptance of modern languages as academic subjects until well into this century, while geography and history were not even recognized as independent secondary school subjects for university entrance purposes until 1939, despite Scotland's legitimate boast, a century earlier, of the comparative width of her curriculum.

At the same time, the laws of commerce being what they are, even the older English universities could not abandon overnight their original, less intelligent or less prestigeful clientele. Reforms at Cambridge did not prove immediately attractive in commercial terms. In 1858, the reforming master of Pembroke, for example, found himself with a total lack of undergraduate entries. Nor did reforms automatically change the nature of such catchment as there was. Rothblatt (1968) has demonstrated that the nature of the families (principally the families of clergy) patronizing Sidney Sussex remained largely constant between 1815 and 1900, while the academic stimulation to the growth of meritocracy supposed to be afforded by the opening up of 'close' scholarships did little, immediately, to encourage a greater influx of intelligent students from schools of lower social status.

Even now, it is doubtful whether Oxford and Cambridge would have abandoned their residual habit of reserving college places for the academically mediocre games-player and the *filius alumni*, or whether Scottish universities would have screened ordinary degree candidates with such care, had not two new economic factors played an ever-increasing part in university development after 1945. The first was, of course, the enormous expansion of research grants and a growth in the availability of money on such a scale that the old economic primacy of caring for the actual teaching of the undergraduates could be largely set aside (except in so far as research itself needed a supply of the most able students). Indeed, it is interesting to see how the departments now most given to defending the high-level teaching of undergraduate classes (as opposed to giving primacy to research) tend to be those, such as philosophy or modern languages, which have not such ready access to large research grants and depend for the adequate staffing of their more elitist and prestigeful activities on the continual existence of a large underbelly of mediocre students.

The second factor was the vast new provision of state aid not only in capital but also in grants to virtually any student that required help. This new wealth ended, finally, any residual dependence on the social elite and created a quite new form of enforced undergraduate elitism as a result of the demand for places. This new elitism is now defended by Cox and Dyson in their *Black Papers* as the natural and 'traditional' elitism of the British university, yet it was most certainly not the natural elitism of Professor Cox's own undergraduate days at Cambridge during the early 1950s when a genuine, intellectual elite could still inhabit the same college with many who would now be considered 'unworthy' of entry to a degree course, or would have to be content with study in some other sector of higher education. University standards (at least at the lower levels) are clearly related to the supply of money.

It is, therefore, perhaps, the ultimate irony that those who defend the elitist sanctum from encroachment should often see as their principal enemy the very state that not only freed the old English universities from sectarian domination, but also freed the British academic from financial anxiety so that, whether as teacher or researcher, he could for the first time pursue his elitist tasks in peace, free from all those earlier economic anxieties that caused Scottish professors to teach and mark singlehanded the work of classes of 600, or caused Oxford tutors to seek out rich or prestigeful games-players of no intellectual distinction in an effort to boost a college building programme.

Typically, it was the state that after 1918 suggested to universities the desirability of establishing the PhD in the light of the general belief (whether ill-founded or not) that Britain was yet again lagging behind America and Germany, and that British universities were, as usual, taking few initiatives to move towards the centre of industrial, let alone general, research activities. In an earlier period most of those who had introduced scientific research into the university sector had studied in Germany or America. Roscoe and Ward had demonstrated at Manchester that a new college that had, like those in London and Durham, failed to catch the market initially could eventually do so by offering an exciting German-style research-based teaching almost entirely new to Britain and destined later to provide a model for a more efficient form of tutorial teaching in Oxford and Cambridge themselves – just as, earlier still, Thomas Jefferson's plans for the University of Virginia (incorporating many German notions) had provided a major model for English curricular expansion in London and elsewhere.

There is then little evidence that the modern homogeneous, academically elitist sector of higher education known as 'universities' could have come into existence without foreign examples and without the state's continuous support and financial protection. In turn the state has always made it clear that such protection has its price in supervision,[6] but given the generally low academic standards of pre-UGC days it is worth considering just how deep-rooted our academic independence and standards would prove to be if this protection were even gradually removed.

Certainly, there is little evidence in the history of the past hundred years to suggest that university elitism is firmly established or that the boundaries between the university and the rest of higher education have been finally and convincingly drawn. We now have a group of elitist university institutions enjoying parity of esteem, and this group is larger than the equivalent group that existed in the 1930s. Yet in many ways the position has hardly changed since then. The low status university colleges, taking London external degrees, have been called to higher service. Instead, we have polytechnics taking the external degrees of the CNAA, whose whole function as a statutory body responsible for supervising the work of scattered colleges is almost exactly that of the pre-1900 University of London, though it trusts the local teachers far more than the earlier body ever did. The Open University also clearly serves many of the categories that the London external degree once served (but with, one hopes, more skilful techniques). The Scottish universities continue to offer a vast number of non-honours degrees chiefly because the different career-structure of that country's teaching profession demands it, so that tasks of general teacher education carried out elsewhere in colleges remain firmly within the university sector.

One can therefore be excused for wondering whether the 'true' functions of the different sectors of higher education are, as yet, clear, and whether firm decisions by apparently autonomous academics in favour of establishing 'centres of excellence' or further sheddings of non-elitist tasks can ever really be effective so long as the old patterns of economic arrangements and the old patterns of sociological development remain largely unexplored beneath the present re-sented but comforting blanket of protection provided by the state. Certainly planning that takes account of such patterns will be far more realistic than any based purely on a false assertion of 'traditional' excellence and a false nostalgia for a late nineteenth-century imperial situation which will never return. University freedom, like artistic freedom, has always depended on the wealthy patron.

Perhaps the state is the only really reliable and tolerant patron we have left.

NOTES

[1] See the report of a speech by the President of the Educational Institute of Scotland in *Educational News*, 24 September 1881, in which he draws attention to complaints from the Rector of the Royal High School about rivalry between school and university.

[2] Noted by Bain in *Educational News*, 13 January 1883.

[3] Only Rothblatt (1968) and McPherson (1973) have made any serious attempt to do so.

[4] Prince Albert's role in university reform has been much underestimated. See Winstanley 1940.

[5] It is amusing to contrast the warmth of the minutes of Court and Senate at Aberdeen in the early part of this century, full of expressions of hope that the university can be of service to professional bodies (whose suggestions are invited and welcomed) with the cold blast that came from the Business Committee of the General Council on 19 October 1935 chiding the EIS and the General Medical Council for attempting to interfere in university affairs.

[6] See, for example, Moody and Beckett (1959) where it is made clear that as early as the Irish Universities Act of 1908 intervention by the Comptroller and the Auditor General in university bookkeeping was envisaged.

REFERENCES

ATTWATER, A. 1939. *Pembroke College, Cambridge*. Cambridge: Cambridge University Press.

BELLOT, HALE. 1929. *University College, London, 1826–1926*. London: Athlone Press.

BOARDMAN, P. 1944. *Patrick Geddes, Maker of the Future*. University of North Carolina Press.

CHARLTON, H. B. 1951. *Portrait of a University*. Manchester: Manchester University Press.

COMMITTEE ON HIGHER EDUCATION. 1963. *Report* (Robbins Report). Cmnd. 2154. London: HMSO.

COX, C. B. and DYSON, A. E. (eds.). 1969. *Fight for education: a Black Paper*. London: Critical Quarterly Society.

DAVIE, G. 1961. *The Democratic Intellect*. Edinburgh: Edinburgh University Press.

HEARNSHAW, F. J. C. 1929. *The Centenary History of King's College, London*. London: Harrap.

LEE, J. 1963. *This Great Journey*. London: MacGibbon and Kee.

MCPHERSON, A. 1973. Selections and Survivals: A Sociology of the Ancient Scottish Universities. In R. K. Brown (ed), *Knowledge, Education, and Cultural Change*. London: Tavistock Publications.

Mind, Vol. 2, p. 74. Philosophy in the Scottish Universities.

MOODY, T. W., and BECKETT, J. C. 1959. *Queen's University, Belfast: The History of a University*. Belfast: Faber and Faber for the University.

ROTHBLATT, S. 1968. *Revolution of the Dons*. London: Faber and Faber.

WHITING, C. E. 1932. *The University of Durham, 1832–1932*. London: Sheldon Press.

WINSTANLEY, H. M. 1935. *Unreformed Cambridge*. Cambridge: Cambridge University Press.

—— 1940. *Early Victorian Cambridge*. Cambridge: Cambridge University Press.

—— 1947. *Late Victorian Cambridge*. Cambridge: Cambridge University Press.

Structure of higher education: some international comparisons

NIGEL GRANT

The formalization of the 'binary system' in Britain did little more than crystallize a feeling, widespread on both sides of the higher educational field, that there was some innate difference between the universities and other kinds of higher institution. Attempts to pin down the distinction, however, have not been conspicuously successful. Some have sought the essence of the 'real university' in unique dedication to learning, based more on wishful thinking than accurate analysis of what actually goes on. Others have suggested some *sine qua non*, insisting that no institution lacking, say, a faculty of divinity can be a 'real university'. Some have even fixed on the very real dual function of higher education – the provision of general *and* professional training – and sought to argue that concern for the theoretical rather than the vocational is characteristic of the university sector,[1] a position rather difficult to maintain in view of the strength in the universities of the overtly vocational faculties of medicine and law. Some have even tried to base the distinction on relationship to the state. One is reminded of the Fleming Committee's difficulties in trying to define a 'public' school; they seemed to agree that it was a uniquely important institution, but were unable to say clearly what it was.

In the hope that looking at other people's practice may help to clarify our own, this paper will consider three of the most prominent working models of higher education in the contemporary world, namely the European (especially the German), the American, and the Soviet higher-educational systems.

1 THE EUROPEAN MODEL

In the European case, one is struck by the prestige of ancient
universities such as the Sorbonne, Lyons, Grenoble, or Heidelberg,
Cologne, or Freiburg. But right away some of the certainties begin
to fade. In France, for instance, the highest prestige is enjoyed not
by the universities so much as by the *grandes écoles* which provide
training for the scientific and administrative elite.[2] These are highly
selective, normally requiring two years' extra preparation after the
baccalauréat. They are small (the *École polytechnique* has only 650
students, compared with the universities' average of over 19,000),
and while the university drop-out rate can be as high as 70 per cent
at times, barely 2 per cent of *grande école* students drop out – they
go, as a rule, *into* the universities. There is nothing quite like this in
Germany, but the universities there do have to share their pedestal
with other types of institution, the professional *Hochschulen* –
generally held to be of similar standing (King 1969). The most
prominent of these are the *technische Hochschulen*, notably those of
Aachen, Berlin, Hanover, and Clausthal; these are normally listed
together with the universities, but the distinction between these and
other types of *Hochschule*, such as the art, music, or medical colleges, is by no means easy to draw in practice – except in the matter
of size, which does not necessarily mean a great deal in itself.

Obviously, some *Hochschulen* enjoy higher esteem than others, a
fact of which the pedagogic academies, among others, are acutely
aware (Whiting 1970). But this cannot be explained in terms of
theoretical as against professional orientation. Some of the philosophical academies, where the curriculum is as theoretical as one
could wish, are not exactly on the pinnacle; the *technische Hochschulen*, by contrast, are supported by the high repute of the engineering profession in Germany. The universities themselves enjoy
the prestige of the medical and legal professions (even more prestigeful than they are here), and the arts and science faculties also benefit
from their vocational associations. Most of their graduates enter
teaching, but a few survive the gruelling obstacle-race of doctorate
and *Habilitation* and, after years of near-medieval apprenticeship
to a professor, gain chairs of their own. Most, however, enter
secondary-school teaching, also a prestigeful profession – there is
a world of difference between the humble *Lehrer* in an elementary
school and *Herr Studienrat* in a *Gymnasium*. In most European

countries, as in nineteenth-century England, the main gap in teaching status is between primary and secondary rather than secondary and higher education. It is significant that most European languages make a clear distinction between teachers of different levels – *Lehrer* and *Studienrat, instituteur* and *professeur,* and so forth. (Interestingly, this is true of the east as well; Rumanian has three distinctive terms, Serbo–Croat no less than four.) In so far as one can distinguish one type of institution from another, the main criterion appears to be professional.

This can hardly be put down to selectivity. In West Germany the 'open-admission' policy is still generally adhered to; possession of the *Abitur* (secondary-school certificate) gives the right of admission to higher education, and although some institutions do now operate a more selective system (based on marks in the *Abitur*), this is simply to save pressure on laboratory space and the like. In the Federal Republic 97 per cent of male *Abiturienten* enter higher education; the figure for women is 85 per cent (Kath, Oehler, and Reichwein 1966). The higher institutions appear socially selective, with overwhelmingly middle-class student bodies, but this is not especially characteristic of the universities, nor in fairness can it be attributed to the institutions themselves. It is at the point of entry to secondary education that selection takes place and this, though ostensibly academic, is strongly class biased. Few are selected (less than 20 per cent on average), and selection is early (age 10 in some states, 12 in others). According to *Wirtschaft und Statistik* (1967) roughly half drop out or fail the *Abitur,* and by the time the survivors have emerged at 19 (minimum) the working-class element has been reduced from some 10 per cent to about 5 per cent. Alternative routes to higher education through the technical-school system account for only 5 per cent of the student body, and have therefore only a marginal effect on its social composition.

The social wastage thus involved has been trounced by one influential author (Picht 1964) as the 'German educational catastrophe'. There have been some steps towards improving the situation. General reform of secondary education is now in the air, and some states have been experimenting with semi-comprehensive structures since the 1950s.[3] Most of these have been hardly radical by British standards – the Berlin 'unified school system', established in the teeth of opposition from traditionalists who saw in it the beginnings of Marxist subversion of the system, was in fact uncannily like the stillborn English tripartite system of the 1940s and would no doubt have been quite acceptable to the authors of the *Black Papers*. Mild though reform has been, however, it has led to an increase in the numbers of potential entrants to higher education, and, predictably, to serious overcrowding. It is now accepted that the higher institutions will have to expand, or become more selective, or both. To some extent, the same problem is being met in France, Scandinavia, and, of course, in Eastern Europe, where post-war comprehensivization of the secondary schools obliged the higher institutions to become more selective years ago.[4]

There are other types of postsecondary provision which, though not strictly speaking part of the higher-educational system in Germany, are nevertheless relevant to it. These *Fachschulen* admit students with lower qualifications than the *Abitur* to vocational courses of about two years' duration. Elsewhere in Europe, however, the trend is towards integrating similar schools into the higher educational system. Filipović (1965) and Grant (1969) point out that the Yugoslavs have long since put their intermediate institutions (called, confusingly enough, *više škole* or higher schools) on the same level as the first two years of the university and equivalent institutions (*visoke škole* or high schools), treating both as the first 'step' of the higher-educational process, from which one may either leave with the first degree or go on to the second step, roughly the equivalent of a British first degree. (The third step is rather like the British postgraduate stage.) Similar developments are now in train or under discussion in East Germany, Rumania, and Bulgaria, among others.[5] Generally, there seems to be a trend towards greater integration of postsecondary education, in which the traditional categories mean progressively less.

If the universities defy clearcut categorization in the teaching field, what about research (claimed by some as the touchstone of real university work)? It is certainly true that this figures large in the preoccupations of most continental universities – the 1959 French law listed this high among the main priorities (Piobetta 1961) – but it is by no means limited to the universities, nor does it generally take precedence over teaching. The reason for this, one suspects, is that the higher educational institutions are not as a rule the most important centres of research, having been upstaged by the specialized research institutes, such as those under the umbrella of the Max-Planck-Gesellschaft in West Germany.

Nor can one generalize too far about the relationship between the universities and the state. State control is the norm, of course, but the degree to which it is exerted varies greatly. In France and Eastern Europe there is close control, even in matters of detail – in Czechoslovakia, for instance, the appointment of every professor has to be approved by the President of the Republic, a power that goes back to well before Svoboda's day (and which is paralleled by our system of Regius chairs). In West Germany, however, the hand of the state rests lightly, in deference to Humboldt's principle of *akademische Freiheit*. The trouble is that freedom is as difficult to define in the academic as in other contexts. For the student, it means freedom to go to classes or not as he wishes, to move from one institution to another, to take examinations when he feels ready, or to drop out if he finds the pace too much (which is what a great many in fact do).[6] For the *Ordinarius*, or professor, it means freedom to teach anything or nothing, and to control the teaching and research of his assistants to an extent that makes the Scottish system seem democratic by contrast. The head of the university, for all his being styled *Rektor Magnificus*, is not in a position to interfere. For the rest of the teaching staff, it is hard to see what freedom they have; the powers of the *Ordinarius* are total. One result of this system is that it is inordinately difficult to reform anything, such as curricula or degree structures. There has long been widespread disquiet over the high drop-out rate, and the length of time even the successful take to complete their courses (nearly seven years on average to complete a four-year course in science, for example, according to Goldschmidt and Sommerkorn 1967). Even the introduction of a first degree has proved difficult. Originally, the first degree was provided by the arts faculty, but when this was absorbed by the *Gymnasium* in the eighteenth century, only the doctorate was left. (Lower qualifications than this are taken by *state* examination.) As so often happens, this relatively late development was incorporated into the ancient tradition, and later suggestions that there might be a place for an MA degree met the opposition of the professors in the older foundations, who saw this as an attack on the traditional excellences of the German university. It has taken the foundation of new universities, such as West Berlin, Konstanz, Bochum, and Bielefeld, to break away from the Ordinarian system and introduce new degrees with more rationally structured courses.[7]

2 THE AMERICAN MODEL

The USA presents a quite different picture, most obviously in the vastly wider range catered for by the higher-educational system. While about 10 per cent of the age-group in Germany enters higher education, in the United States the figure is nearer 50 per cent according to the US Office of Education's 1970 figures. Admittedly, the two are not strictly comparable; much American college work is more like that of a German *Gymnasium* than a *Hochschule*. But the *Gymnasium* accounts for a relatively small proportion of the age-group in any case; when all due allowances are made, we are still left with a great spread of colleges, enough to make it clear that they are not, as a category, academically or socially elite institutions in the European sense.

All that the American higher institutions have in common is that they are postsecondary, they vary in practically every other respect. There are specialized colleges like California Institute of Oriental Studies, vast general institutions like the University of California, engineering institutions like Caltech, teachers' colleges, liberal arts colleges, seminaries, colleges with strong or weak religious links as the case may be, and, of course, institutions reckoned to be of outstanding quality and others that are not. Out of this multiplicity it is not easy to determine what are universities; most institutions that call themselves by that name do tend to have a wide range of courses and a particular concern with general education, but so do many liberal arts colleges, while many universities clearly see themselves as having a specialized role.

The variation in size is particularly striking.[8] Even leaving aside the multicampus giants such as the State University of New York with 261,000 students, on the one hand, and tiny colleges such as the Mennonite Biblical Seminary (Elkhart, Indiana) with 45, on the other, we can find within the single state of Ohio twenty-two universities, from Ohio State (Columbus) with 35,000 students to Wilberforce University (Xenia) with under 1,000. Most non-Americans tend to think of the typical American college as a massive institution like, say, Penn State or Berkeley, Chicago or Wisconsin. These are certainly conspicuous, but they are not typical. Leaving aside the junior colleges, together with those colleges and universities not recognized by accrediting bodies (Ian Paisley's alma mater, Bob Jones, is probably the best known of these), we can reduce the figure of some 2,400 institutions to some 1,100. Of these, many come into the giant category – nearly 5 per cent with over 20,000 students, 12 per cent with over 10,000. But the majority are much smaller than Edinburgh: three-quarters have fewer than 5,000 students, over half have fewer than 2,000 and 30 per cent have under 1,000. The average is around 4,500. Nor is there much connection between size and quality or prestige, however determined. True, Berkeley has 25,000 and Columbia 17,000, but then Kent State has 27,000, and is not exactly at the top of the pecking order. Contrariwise, Vassar has 1,600, Princeton around 4,000, while many other 'prestige schools', public and private, have between 5,000 and 8,000. Massachusetts Institute of Technology, for example, has just over 7,000 students. It would seem that the massive growth of tertiary education in America should be attributed not so much to the expansion of the 'multiversities' as to the nationwide proliferation of small and middle-sized colleges and universities.

Faced with the range of American higher institutions, and a common career structure for the whole, some commentators have attempted to determine what proportion of young Americans go to 'real' universities. After all, the standards required to become accredited colleges are still far from exacting, since they include Ivy League and major state institutions in the same category as Corpus Christi University, Texas (student population 550) which, according to the *New York Times* (11 January 1967), advertizes 'sun, surf and sand' as its main attractions. Whether one is trying to demonstrate the awfulness of most American higher education, or to show that the majority do in fact go to good schools, is immaterial; the exercise, so far, has been quite futile. Subjectivity, and the degree of intra- as well as intercollege variation, see to that. Further, most higher institutions see the provision of broad general courses as part of their function; the fact that much of this could be reasonably compared with that done in an English sixth form let alone a German *Gymnasium* or a French *lycée*, does not necessarily affect the standing of the institution itself. They all have to take as their starting-point the level of high-school graduation which, with the exception of students who have taken Advance Placement Program papers,[9] is usually modest by European standards. (American high schools rarely see striving for high-level academic attainment as part of their job; their function is at least as much social as academic.) With few exceptions, what gives a university or college prestige is what happens at the other end of the process, that is, effective graduate and professional schools. With the burgeoning of graduate schools in what used to be simply four-year undergraduate colleges, this too is becoming increasingly difficult to assess. One is always hearing of the grotesque PhDs in driver education or sport, and it is common knowledge that there are some universities whose higher degrees are at least as good as any taken in Europe. The extremes are easy enough to distinguish; the difficulty, as usual, is in knowing where to draw the line in between.

Even the quality of teaching faculty, however one determines that, is not always a reliable guide to the standing of an institution. There are, once again, some about whose quality there is no dispute. But many relatively mediocre universities have found that money can be well spent in establishing a number of special appointments, suitably ballasted with high salaries and research grants, which will tempt a few 'big names', to come, at least for a while, and help raise the general level.

Nor, common mythology to the contrary, can much be deduced from the relationship with the state. Most of the oldest institutions, the 'respectably ancient', are private foundations; Harvard, Yale, William and Mary, Princeton, were all in operation before the end of the eighteenth century. But, for what it is worth, so were some state universities, such as Georgia or North Carolina. Again, it is true that the great universities whose names spring most readily to mind are private schools like Harvard, Yale, or Columbia, but can anyone seriously argue that such state universities as California, Michigan, or Penn State are not in the same league? Conversely, the undistinguished or downright poor colleges are also, more often than not, private. (This is not to argue any necessary disadvantage in private control either – it just so happens that there are many more private institutions, 1,472 as compared with 1,011 public ones. It also happens that the position is reversed as far as student numbers is concerned: 2,036,000 private as against 4,892,000 public (US Office of Education figures). But, as we have seen, numbers mean little either way.) There undoubtedly exists, in some quarters, a social preference for private colleges, but this is no more a guarantee of quality than the preference of some British parents for private schools. State interference is associated in many minds with such actions as those of Governor Reagan in California, which is certainly one form interference can take; but the regents of a private university, backed by business interests and influential alumni, can be quite as constricting as any politician, and less accountable. In many cases, in fact, the role of the state in maintaining standards has been of some importance.

The most obvious division between different kinds of post-secondary education cuts right across the criteria so far mentioned, namely, that between junior and senior colleges. The function of junior colleges – one of growing importance – is to provide two-year courses from which one can emerge with an associate's degree (AA and AS) or else go on to a senior institution to complete the more familiar bachelor's degree. Variation of this kind is on the increase at the other end of the process too, as witness the growing tendency to make available new degrees (like the Yale MPh) for the course-work part of the PhD programme.[10] The logic of greater segmentation of this kind is more mobility between different kinds of institution, and a further blurring of the boundaries between them.

There does seem to be one sense in which the universities dominate the scene. The word is attached to most (though not all) of the most prestigeful institutions; the less eminent often feel it worth their while to change their titles from institute or college to university as a sign that they have arrived (Kent State is an example of this). This may reflect broadening of function, growth of numbers, raising of standards – or it may not. Alternatively, many smaller colleges, teachers' or liberal arts colleges as a rule, feel that they gain by absorption into one of the multicampus structures like New York State or Missouri, California or North Carolina. In this sense, 'university' seems to mean something. But what, precisely? It seems to carry some weight, but stubbornly defies definition. Perhaps it would be better to settle for the common American practice of using 'university', 'college', and 'school' more or less interchangeably, and to recognize that the American system is not so much a graduated hierarchy as a continuum. One may plot points of excellence on it, but drawing clearcut boundaries simply does not work.

3 THE SOVIET MODEL

One way of annoying Americans and Russians impartially is to suggest that in education (as in much else) they have more in common than either cares to admit. Though it is the distinctive features that we are concerned with here, it is worth noting that they share one basic assumption, namely that the concept of mass education applies to the tertiary as well as the primary and secondary stages. The ways they go about it, however, differ enormously.

The Soviet system is, unlike the American, centralized. There are, needless to say, no private institutions of any kind. The educational system as a whole comes under two ministries at union level; broadly speaking, the Ministry of Education of the USSR looks after the general schools, while the Ministry of Higher Education is responsible for the higher institutions. (This arrangement is repeated in each of the constituent republics, but this need not detain us here – the degree of effective devolution is not great.) Actually, the system is a good deal less neat than it may appear, since many of the higher institutions come under the more immediate oversight of other ministries. The music conservatories come under the Ministry of Culture, the medical institutes under the Ministry of Health, and so on, with the Ministry of Higher Education exercising a general supervisory role.[11] The extent of control goes far beyond anything the University Grants Committee would (one assumes) even dream of, right down to the number of hours per subject per week in every year of every course. Even the number of essays, tests, and examinations is prescribed in the official 'instructional plans'. Some institutions have their own 'individual plans', but only with ministerial approval.

Soviet higher education, building on the nineteenth-century German tradition of professional Hochschulen, has carried specialization about as far as it can go. Most professional training is provided not in the universities, but in specialized institutions at comparable level; doctors and dentists, engineers and technologists, lawyers and economists receive their training in medical, technical, legal, and other institutes. The role of the universities is limited to what is left, that of providing courses in the humanities and the pure sciences. Some of the graduates become research workers or the like, the majority, however, join their counterparts from the pedagogic institutes teaching in the secondary schools.

Thus, the universities occupy a much smaller part of the higher educational system than they do in Britain. There are 794 higher-educational institutions (vysshie uchebnye zavedeniya, hence the useful abbreviation VUZ). Of these, only 45 are styled universities. Actually, since they tend to be fairly large institutions (over 7,000 students on average) their share is greater than this figure might suggest. Still, with 7·3 per cent of the total student body and 7·9 per cent of the graduates, they form one of the minor categories. By way of contrast, the various types of technical and polytechnical institute account for no less than 44·1 per cent of the students and 38·1 per cent of the graduates.[12]

Officially, there is no gap in standard or esteem between the universities and other *VUZy*. Since they are subject to the same kind of governmental control, one of the props of our binary system is missing; they are also organized internally in much the same way. In many minor but possibly symbolically important respects there is little to choose between them. All have such titles as professor and reader for senior academic staff. The system of degree nomenclature is the same. Nor, once again, do the universities dominate the research field. It is true that their contribution is out of proportion to their share of the higher educational sector, but research is carried on in all types of *VUZ*, notably the larger technical institutes. Nor are the universities the pinnacle of the research pyramid; this is to be found not in the higher-educational institutions at all, but in the special research institutes, notably those attached to the Academy of Sciences of the USSR. The same is true of higher-degree work. Wherever they are taken, there are two kinds of higher degree – Candidate of Sciences (roughly equivalent to our PhD) and Doctor of Sciences (more like a British or French higher doctorate). The latter is much less commonly awarded; there are only 20,000 of them at present, compared with 186,000 Candidates.

Strictly speaking, higher degrees are not awarded by the *VUZy* at all, but by the Ministry. An institution can make a recommenda- tion, but this has to be confirmed by the Ministry's Higher Quali- fications Commission or VAK (*vysshaya attestatsionnaya kommis- siya*). Work for higher degrees, therefore, need not take place in the higher-educational institutions at all, let alone the universities. Of the 98,000 postgraduates currently enrolled for higher-degree work, 56,000 are studying in *VUZy*, the rest in scientific research institutes. Incidentally, there is no suggestion that such degrees taken outside a *VUZ* are in any way inferior to those taken internally; the *VAK*, after all, has to approve them in either case.

Whether one is considering organization or administration, teaching or research, all classes of *VUZ* are legally equal. But in practice some are more equal than others, and some less. It is probably true that the universities as a group enjoy greater prestige

than most other institutions. Conversely, many of the smaller pedagogic institutes are widely regarded as 'second-class institutions',
and often find it difficult to compete with other *VUZy* in attracting
staff and students of high calibre.[13] But one should not make too
much of this, for the differences are greater between individual
institutions than between categories. The universities of Moscow
and Leningrad have an unparalleled reputation, and places in them
are greatly sought after. But engineering is one of the most highly
regarded professions in the USSR, and such *VUZy* as the Kalinin
Polytechnic in Leningrad or the Riga Polytechnic or, for that matter,
the IM Glubkin Oil and Chemical Gas Industries Institute (Order
of the Red Banner of Labour) in Moscow enjoy a reputation greater
than that of many universities. Nor are the pedagogic institutes
uniformly low in esteem; the Herzen Institute in Leningrad, the
Lenin Institute in Moscow, the foreign language pedagogic institutes
there and in Gorki and Minsk, are quite a different proposition from
the more remote 'mini-institutes', and are more highly esteemed
than the universities of, say, Yakutsk or Dushambe. These institutes
share with some of the more prominent universities the right to their
own 'individual instructional plans', which is not lightly conceded
by the Ministry. Once again, though one can detect differences in
reputation and standards (though the two do not necessarily co-
incide), there is no clearcut division between the universities as a
whole and other kinds of higher-educational institution.

There is wide distinction, however, between the higher institutions
on the one hand and the *tekhnikumy* or secondary specialized schools
on the other. Although not officially part of the higher-educational
system, they do some of the work assigned to parts of the higher
systems elsewhere. This may be described as 'lower professional'
training; they provide courses in music, art, librarianship, clerical
work, nursing, transport, and communications, and a wide range of
qualifications in engineering and technology. They also train the
majority of primary-school teachers and practically all kindergarten
teachers. Courses last for four years for those entering at 15, two
for those coming in after completing the general school at 17 or so;
at present, then, they overlap the secondary and tertiary stages. It is
possible that as a consequence of current secondary-school changes
they may move completely into the postsecondary stage – since they
come under the same ministry as the *VUZy*, the machinery is already
there – but this is not likely in the immediate future.[14] These schools

are already an important sector of the educational system. They have slightly fewer students than the *VUZy* (4,262,000 as against 4,470,000), but due to their shorter courses they release a much larger number of graduates per year (902,800 compared with 510,000 from the *VUZy*). Unfortunately, the figures do not distinguish the secondary from the postsecondary entrants, but the indications are that what began as a variant of the trade school has been turning into a sort of professional junior college. How far this process will continue remains to be seen.

The USSR has, like the other systems mentioned so far, had to meet growing pressure on higher-education from the rapid expansion of the secondary schools. Open entry on the German model was given up long ago; under the present system, all applicants have to take a competitive entrance examination regardless of their attainment in the school-leaving examinations. The ratio of applicants to places varies a great deal, but in general an applicant has, at best, a one in three chance of getting in (Prokofiev 1966). Khrushchev attempted to take off some of the pressure by giving preference to the *stazhniki*, those who had worked in production for at least two years, but this was not conspicuously successful and is now largely in abeyance. A longer established way of alleviating the pressure is the extensive use of parttime courses (though there are financial, manpower, and even ideological reasons for this as well). The parttime contingent has been fluctuating during the last two decades. Between 1950 and 1960 it rose from 43·6 per cent of the total number of entrants to 56·6 per cent, but in the last ten years it has been going down again. In 1968 fulltime entrants were once again in the majority (51 per cent). It seems that, whatever their advantages, parttime courses are less efficient. They take a year longer in theory, more in practice; they are generally admitted to attain lower standards; and they are much more liable to suffer from drop out. Parttimers, even when they were a majority of all students, have consistently made up a minority of the graduates. Drop-out rates vary from place to place, but one study (Rutkevich 1965), based on all the *VUZy* in Sverdlovsk, showed an average of 5·3 per cent per year – over a quarter of the student body during the five-year course. (In some departments, it was as high as 10 per cent per year.) Parttimers, however, were particularly vulnerable – 12·7 per cent per year for those in correspondence classes, 14·3 per cent per year for evening classes. The *stazhniki* did badly as well, losing 45·6 per cent of their number during the five-year course. Although it would be rash to generalize too far from the Sverdlovsk study, it is generally conceded that over the country as a whole between a fifth and a quarter of those entering the first-year course do not take the final diploma. This is not bad when compared with some other countries, but it does cast doubt on the selection procedure, and has given rise to much heart-searching over the need to improve parttime courses, integrate them more effectively with the students' normal work, improve teaching methods, and, for good measure, to a governmental inspection of all *VUZy* in the USSR.[15] This, however, will take years to complete at the present rate, according to Krupin (1969).

The problems of Soviet higher education, however, are those of the system as a whole rather than any one category. There are some difficulties of demarcation, especially between the universities and the pedagogic institutes, both of which train secondary-school teachers. Since teacher training is an integral part of most university courses, since most university graduates go, often reluctantly, into the schools, and since the better pedagogic institutes take the professional side more seriously than the universities do, there is some uncertainty what the university is for (Mikhalev 1965, Dubinina & Slepenkov 1965). In vocational terms, the answer appears to be a rather more specialized version of teacher training, with the ablest minority being creamed off into research or something similar. It would be idle to pretend that the universities derive their status from the actual destination of most of their graduates (as do the technical institutes); it comes, instead, from the destination of the minority, to which the majority also aspire. There is, of course, ample precedent for this elsewhere; only in the Soviet Union is it quite so obvious and extreme.

4 CONCLUSIONS

What emerges from these case studies is that although in every system there is some general concept of 'university', it is often ill-defined and difficult to distinguish unambiguously from other kinds of post-secondary education. From one country to another, there is little in common but the name. The role of the university is inclusive in the USA and residual in the USSR, while other systems show various intermediate positions.

Least of all can one characterize the university as the general, non-vocational institution. Rather, where universities enjoy a special esteem, this can be associated with that of the professions that draw upon them. Where prestigeful professions are provided for elsewhere, the institutions associated with them have high prestige also. Nor is there much future in looking for inherent academic respectability in university-based professions that the others somehow lack; it needs more evidence than is usually offered to carry conviction that law, medicine, or, nowadays, business, are theoretically richer or intellectually more demanding than, say, agriculture or pedagogy or the visual arts. It is much more likely that there is a connection between the social prestige of a profession in a particular society and the regard in which its feeder schools are held.

In the international context, the British binary system, with its insistence on treating the university as a qualitatively different kind of institution, begins to look rather parochial. It may be none the worse for that – minorities can be right – but this has to be based on argument, not assumption. The equation of the 'real university', or even 'real higher education', with the kind of university we happen to be familiar with rests on neither comparative nor historical evidence. Perhaps our own tribal customs do have some value, but it is not enhanced by treating them as if they were laws of nature.

NOTES

¹ See, for example, James 1949, Chap. 3.
² See, for example, King 1967, Chap. 4, and Halls 1965, Chap. 9.
³ The *Einheitsschule*, or 'unified school system', was not really a comprehensive system at all; by postponing the age of entry to the *Gymnasium* from 10 to 12 years of age, however, and by transforming the old terminal elementary classes into a practically biased secondary school, it ensured that all pupils at least entered secondary education, and did so at the same age. Transfer from one type of school to another, while not common, became at least possible, and a somewhat higher proportion of the age-group was admitted to academic secondary courses than in the more traditional systems in many other states of the Federal Republic. See Enderwitz (1963). For a later (and critical) assessment see Robinson and Kuhlman (1967).
⁴ See Grant 1969, Chaps. 6 and 8.
⁵ See E. G. Geisel 1966, Apostolescu 1966, and Zhivkov 1969.

[6] Drop-out rates vary enormously. In the more highly structured vocational courses, they are relatively low – 6 per cent of men and 19 per cent of women in pharmacology, for example, or 13 per cent and 29 per cent respectively in medicine. In the more general courses, however, they can be much higher – 24 and 42 per cent in economics and social sciences, and 45 and 63 per cent in the humanities. See Kath *et al.* 1966, p. 175. Figures analysed in Goldschmidt and Sommerkorn 1967.

[7] For a case study see Brezinka 1967. See also King 1969.

[8] Raw figures are from *The World of Learning 1969–70*, which lists all accredited higher institutions, with enrolments.

[9] The standard of an Advanced Placement Program paper is roughly that of a Scottish first ordinary pass, and entitles the student to certain exemptions at university. These programmes are taken by about two per cent of the age-group.

[10] These are sometimes known as 'Candidate' or 'ABD' (all but dissertation) degrees. See Springer 1968. The practice of recognizing individual course-credits for qualification and salary purposes in the teaching profession is well established in many states.

[11] Over twenty Ministries and other bodies control higher educational institutions, under the general supervision of the Ministry of Higher and Secondary Specialized Education of the USSR. Institutions are listed, with their responsible Ministries, in Ministerstvo vysshego i srednego spetsial'nogo obrazovaniya SSSR: *Spravochnik dlya postupayushchikh v vuzy SSSR v 1970 godu* (Vysshayshkola, Moscow, 1970).

[12] Raw figures from *Narodnoe khozyaistvo SSSR v 1968 godu: statisticheskii yezhegodnik* (Statistika, Moscow, 1969), from which all Soviet figures are taken unless otherwise stated. For a fuller account, see Grant 1971.

[13] See Mikhalev (1965) and the article Slovo pedagogicheskomu vuzu (1967).

[14] Ten-year schooling (age 7–17) is now obligatory in the USSR. Although this is normally provided in the ten-year general school, some pupils still go into secondary specialized or vocational schools after the eighth form (age 15). When the present policy was being outlined in 1966, the Minister of Education expected that about 25 per cent of the age-group would do this. See Prokofiev 1966.

[15] See Bogomolov 1969 and A. V. Krupin 1969.

REFERENCES

A chto zhe togda universitet? (no author). *Uchitel'skaya gazeta*, 2 August 1965.

APOSTOLESCU, NICOLAE. 1966. Orientarea învăţămîntului universitar şi pedagogic superior. *Lupta de Clasă* 1.

Structure of higher education: some international comparisons 45

BOGOMOLOV, A. I. 1969. Povyshat' kachestvo podgotovki zaochnikov i vechernikov. *Vestnik vysshei shkoly* 8: 3–8.

BREZINKA, WOLFGANG. 1967. The University of Konstanz: An Attempt to reform the German University. In *The University within the Educational System* (Proceedings of the Comparative Education Society in Europe): 183–200. Ghent.

DUBININA, I. S., and SLEPENKOV, I. M. 1965. Universitet -uchitel' – shkola. *Vestnik vysshei shkoly* 3: 15–18.

ENDERWITZ, HERBERT. 1963. Two German Educational Reform Schemes: the Rahmenplan and the Bremerplan. *Comparative Education Review* 7 (1): 47–50.

FILIPOVIĆ, MARIJAN. 1965. *Higher Education in Yugoslavia.* Belgrade: Medjunarodna Politika.

GEISEL, KURT. 1966. Reform des Hochschulwesens. *Informationsdienst zum Bildungswesen in Osteuropa* 12–13: 85–93.

GOLDSCHMIDT, DIETRICH and SOMMERKORN, INGRID N. 1967. Transmission from School to University in West Germany. In *The University within the Educational System* (Proceedings of the Comparative Education Society in Europe) 59–78. Ghent.

GRANT, NIGEL. 1969. *Society, Schools and Progress in Eastern Europe.* London: Pergamon.

GRANT, NIGEL. 1971. *Soviet Education.* Harmondsworth: Penguin.

JAMES, ERIC. 1949. *An Essay on the Content of Education.* London: Harrap.

KATH, OEHLER, and REICHWEIN. 1966. Studienweg und Studienerfolg. In Institut für Bildungsforschung *Studien und Berichte* 6: 175.

KING, E. J. 1967. *Other Schools and Ours.* New York: Holt, Rinehart and Winston.

KING, E. J. 1969. *Education and Development in Western Europe.* New York: Addison-Wesley.

KRUPIN, A. V. 1969. Gosudarstvennoe inspektirovanie vuzov. *Vestnik vysshei shkoly* 11: 3–7.

MIKHALEV, G. M. 1965. Sovershenstvovat' podgotovku pedagogicheskikh kadrov. *Sovietskaya pedagogika* 6: 104–9.

PICHT, GEORG. 1964. *Die deutsche Bildungskatastrophe.* Walter-Verlag.

PIOBETTA, J.-B. 1961. *Les institutions universitaires en France.* Paris: Presses Universitaires de France.

PROKOFIEV, M. A. 1966. Segodnya i zavtra nashei shkoly. *Pravda,* 12 December 1966.

ROBINSOHN, SAUL B. and KUHLMAN, CASPAR. 1967. Two Decades of Non-reform in West German Education. *Comparative Education Review* 40 (3): 311–30.

RUTKEVICH, M. N. 1965. *Vestnik vysshei shkoly* 7.

Slovo pedagogicheskomu vuzu (no author). *Uchitel'skaya gazeta,* 9 February 1969.

SPRINGER, GEORGE F. 1968. Universities in Flux. *Comparative Education Review* 12 (1): 28–38.

WHITING, CHARLES. 1970. Integration of Teacher Training. *The Times Educational Supplement* (Scotland), 27 November 1970.

Wirtschaft und Statistik 9 (1967): 521.

ZHIVKOV, TODOR. 1969. *Rabotničesko delo*, 1 August 1969.

Role of the new universities

T. L. COTTRELL

By the 'new universities' I understand the new institutions created in the United Kingdom during the last decade, and given full university status (that is degree-giving powers) at their inception. These universities are East Anglia, Essex, Kent, Lancaster, Sussex, Warwick, and York in England, Stirling in Scotland, and the University of Ulster at Coleraine in Northern Ireland. With these must be associated in some respects the University of Keele, which was in many ways their precursor. Keele, however, was the successor of the University College of North Staffordshire which was founded as long ago as 1949. Its growth was fairly slow during its first few years, and it did not originally have full university powers. To the list should perhaps also be added The Open University, which was founded with full powers at its outset but which is really a totally different sort of institution.

The new universities were created with two main objects in mind: first, to allow expansion, that is to provide more university places; and second, it was hoped that they might be centres of innovation in university education.

Having in mind their role in increasing the number of places available, the new universities were established on out-of-town sites where there was not likely to be any serious obstacle to expansion, in the form of other buildings close by. As a consequence of this decision to go for fairly remote sites residential accommodation is likely to be a more serious problem in these institutions than in some of the older ones, where there is a greater possibility of students living at home.

I should like to consider the extent to which new universities have been able to fulfil the functions implicit in the reasons for their foundation. Their first function was to supply places. Slight disappointment has been expressed in some quarters about the relatively small contribution made by the new universities to the expansion of number of places available in the 1960s. For example, a report on the expansion of higher education in 1970–80 prepared by the National Union of Students in 1970 discusses the establishment of the 'new universities' in the 1960s and, relating exclusively to the English situation, they remark:

> the contribution, in terms of numbers, to the over-doubling of university places in ten years which these institutions have made has not been substantial (14,200 places out of the total growth of 94,600), although it is accepted that in the future having been established they could now bear a much greater share of expansion in total figures than heretofore.

Although the observation is correct, there seems to be no particular reason for disappointment in view of the length of time involved in setting up a new university, particularly if the second objective, that of academic innovation, is borne in mind. However, the following figures may help to put the position in perspective. The entry to the new universities (as listed above), for the 1968–69 session was 6,839 students or 8·2 per cent of the UK total. Again the total number of undergraduate students in the new universities in that year was 12,633 (7·1 per cent of the UK total) and of postgraduate students was 2,236 or 5·8 per cent of the UK total. This is a considerable achievement in view of the fact that of the nine institutions concerned, one had been taking students for only one year and another for only two, and that taken together they represent just under 20 per cent of the total number of university institutions.

It seems clear from these figures that the new universities have succeeded as far as the provision of places is concerned, and have in fact achieved very high growth-rates. This has had some intriguing results. In the first place, a high physical growth-rate has required fairly sophisticated managerial planning. This is not to say that all universities in present circumstances do not require such planning; they do. It is to say, however, that the nature of the situation forced this planning on new institutions. One thinks of the development plan for York, for Warwick, and for Stirling. One thinks of the study made of the managerial function and the planning function at the University of Sussex; one thinks of the operational research studies on models of university growth at Lancaster; and, while I would not wish to draw attention to any specific features of the situation in Stirling, the network analysis of its start-up embodied both physical and academic considerations that were interesting to work out. Thus, one consequence of the rapid expansion required has been an increased interest in university managerial techniques. However, this is not a necessary consequence of founding a new university; in fact, I understand from those who were at Keele in the early days that many managerial problems were at first treated in a very unsystematic way.

One consequence of the rather tight planning imposed at the outset has been that the new universities have achieved an architectural unity, and in some cases distinction, which has tended to be lacking in many older institutions, most of which possess fine buildings, often in somewhat random juxtaposition. One thinks of the unified university schemes, with residence related carefully to the rest of the university, of Denys Lasdun at East Anglia and of Kenneth Capon at Essex, and the peaceful but slightly suburban atmosphere of York created by Robert Matthew, Johnson-Marshall, and Partners.

There are other, perhaps less satisfactory, consequences of a rapid growth-rate. I should perhaps explain in terms of a specific institution what I mean by 'rapid'. In Stirling over the last four years the undergraduate student population has doubled every year, the numbers being 150, 300, 600, and 1,200. It is an interesting comment on the difficulties of planning that we did not in fact intend this. Our original plan over these four years was for slower expansion: 150, 300, 450, and 1,125. This involved a doubling in the second year, but not to a very large number, followed by a year of consolidation when the increase was only 50 per cent, and then slightly more than doubling in the fourth year. In both cases the number in the fourth year is fairly large in relation to that in the preceding year. This was because a large number of students was necessary in order to justify the number of staff needed to provide an adequate coverage for final-year (that is, fourth-year) students in all the subjects we taught. The number this year had to be increased even beyond what we originally thought necessary if we were to attain the target set for the quinquennium by the University Grants Committee. This emphasizes the managerial difficulty of planning in an 'autonomous' institution whose overall size and object are determined from time to time by an outside body.

The rapid growth-rate produces two sorts of strain. First, the university population puts pressure on the physical assets, so that a delay in building completion can cause severe difficulties, if existing accommodation is already fully used and if further expansion is inherent in the situation. Such delays have occurred in many new universities, notably in Essex, East Anglia, and Stirling.

While being seriously concerned with academic innovation, the problem for new universities of coping with building delays is severe at all times and most pressing at around the time the first students graduate, which is when academic problems tend to reach their most obvious definition – how successful new courses have been, and whether and how they should be changed.

It is arguable that new universities have slightly more than their random share of what is sometimes known as student unrest. This may well be because rapid expansion results in a higher proportion of the university community being strangers to one another than would be the case in a less rapidly expanding situation. It may also be that irritations related to lack of buildings completed spill over into other fields. Indeed it may relate to the fact that no other universities but Stirling have *all* their buildings built to the current University Grants Committee norms and cost standards. If there is much student residence on the university campus, some members of the university are spending their entire time in buildings whose standards of space, style, and finish have been severely cost limited. For example, it has been put to me by students at Stirling that it is very important that we should retain a Victorian hotel building which we own in Bridge of Allan nearby so as to allow students the experience of enjoying the space-standards of an earlier age.

Nevertheless, although rapid growth of student populations has created problems, it is clear that the new universities have fulfilled their first requirement of providing places.

We come now to the second, subsidiary, reason for their existence: the possibilities for innovation in university education.

In the first place, I think we ought to note that there is some conflict between rapid growth and innovation. The assumption is frequently made that the pressures on the education system are so great that the available university places will always be filled. This is broadly true, apart from instances of certain specific subjects, but it is also desirable that places should be filled with a due proportion of academically able students. However, it seems likely that a number of academically able students, particularly in the sciences, may fall into the class that Professor Hudson has described as 'convergers', i.e. tend not to go to new universities, or, if they do, tend not to try new courses. This means even mildly radical academic innovations may conflict with rapid growth, not so much because of the managerial difficulties caused, but because of reluctance of able but conventional students to participate in innovatory courses. I think it is possible that some of the early difficulties experienced by Keele may have been caused by resistance to the novelty of the foundation year on the one hand, and the abandonment of the single-subject honours degree on the other. I think that the history of the other new universities tends to show that innovation by itself is not enough; to be successful it must be accompanied by a substantial campaign to make known the merits of the particular change.

With this proviso, let us have a rather impressionist look at what has been done, and not done, in the way of innovation. Since the new universities have not so far got round to publishing assessments of their innovations, my comments must be incomplete.

In the first place, let us look at what they have not done. I think it is fairly obvious that, although some of them have tackled the managerial aspects of running a university, there has been little change in the governmental structure of the new universities. They have all adhered to the traditional two-tier system of an academic body, or Senate, and a supreme governing body, or Council (Court, in Scotland), comprising some academics and some laymen, with power to make decisions on all aspects of the university's policy, other than academic. It seems to me that this structure, workable though it obviously is, is subject to reasonable criticism from two points of view. First, by formally separating the academic from the financial and physical aspects of the university, it creates a dual structure in which financial responsibility is not very directly associated with executive responsibility. In other words, it could be argued that the structure is unsound from a managerial point of view. The other line of attack is to say that the university is essentially an academic community and that there are therefore two things wrong with the structure. The first thing is that the main governing body should not be a body substantially composed of laymen because they do not properly understand universities. This criticism is often averted, and I fear with some success in certain universities, by saying that although the Council is formally the supreme governing body, in practice it does whatever the Senate says it should do. More importantly, according to the syndicalist academic view, the Senate itself usually consists of senior academics and neither junior academics nor students have nearly enough say in the running of the university.

On the whole, academic planning boards of new universities seem to have paid more attention to the second criticism. They have been at pains to diffuse, if not executive power, at least consultation fairly widely throughout the academic staff. Several of them, for example, have an academic assembly that can debate and put forward recommendations on any matter concerning the university. Originally, however, none of the new universities made much move in the direction of including students in their governing bodies. This is an interesting fact. All these new universities, mostly set up in the early 1960s, had academic planning boards consisting of individuals experienced in a variety of universities, and interested in creating new ones. Because they were responsible for preparing the draft charters and statutes of the new institutions they had every incentive to think hard about university government, and not one of them put students into a position of any strength in the university governmental system. I do not know whether it never occurred to them, or whether it did and they rejected it. And yet, less than ten years later, we have a Select Committee of the House of Commons making recommendations in this direction. This failure, if failure it be, in innovation, shows that the new universities concerned were not only having to cope with rapid changes in physical growth, but also with a rapid change in the climate of external opinion about who should run a university. It is again interesting to remember that some of the new universities created in the nineteenth century were at pains to ensure that even the professoriat had as little formal control as possible over the destiny of the institution. The current move towards syndicalism is, then, an important one, which on the whole finds the new universities in an intermediate and not very happy position.

What about academic innovation? Keele, as I have already mentioned made substantial changes; other universities, notably Sussex, emphasized interdisciplinary studies in an effort to give them the status that a departmental organization seemed to forbid them. Thus at Keele, Sussex, and Stirling among others the interrelatedness of knowledge has been emphasized in an attempt to restrict what was often regarded as the 'excessive' specialization of more traditional universities.

How far has this major trend away from specialization and in favour of interdisciplinary work proceeded? Within the departmental structure, it has been successful, for example, operational research at Lancaster and Sussex, and industrial science in Stirling. The foundation year at Keele continues as an example, albeit not very widely followed, to us all. I find that I know of only one direct failure (and in view of people's reticence about their failures this is perhaps hardly surprising), which is the Stirling course called 'Approaches and Methods'. This was a course on general intellectual methods aimed at all students. It dealt with logic, elementary social arithmetic and computers, and scientific method. This course was worked out by a group of four professors, and was taught over three years to the entire first year of the university. Initially students were hostile, later they became resigned rather than enthusiastic. Initially most academic staff were enthusiastic, but eventually they became hostile. From an academic point of view the course was only moderately satisfactory. On the other hand, it went totally against the grain of the modern academic ethos of specialist expertise, and it has been discontinued.

At Stirling we are also doing something that, although not unique, is unusual: a combined course in education and other subjects. This was done at Keele, where the two-subject honours degree made it particularly easy to carry out. At Stirling it was difficult to find subjects that were prepared to allow for education the amount of time that the education department thought appropriate to the new degree, and at present we cover mathematics, biology, and history only. We hope to expand these in the near future to include French and German, but courses have not been worked out in detail as yet. I do not want to go into the academic details of either 'Approaches and Methods' or the education course; I should like to note that from my experience in Stirling it is clear that even in a new university conservative academic forces are very strong indeed, particularly where new proposals are for courses that cross subject boundaries.

New proposals being worked out in the context of a single subject, however, usually are not too difficult to bring into effect. Here the general conservatism of the academic outlook is an asset to innovation rather than a liability in the sense that if the professor of a given subject wants to teach it differently, he can appoint staff who, he hopes, will agree with him, and arrange the course more or less to suit himself. Then, in dealing with those who question his judgement he has, in the last resort, the very powerful claim that in the academic context he is the professional in this field. This gives him fairly wide scope for innovation in course contact and teaching method, though perhaps not in examination and assessment. Therefore my experience suggests that when innovation is sought within established disciplines, a new university is a very powerful institution in achieving it. On the other hand, if a movement is made towards interdisciplinary courses even in a new institution the difficulties are considerable.

Finally, it may be worth making an observation on another aspect of the formation and growth of new universities. We live at a time when a self-consciously proclaimed youth culture is attempting to separate the young from the accumulated traditions of the rest of the community – this tendency is most obvious among the intelligent young who attend universities. The new universities, set up before this phenomenon was fully appreciated, have been located in places where few students can live at home and so the majority live in their own student communities, either in university residences on the campus or in lodgings or flats nearby. This means that at a time when we have already a divisiveness of outlook among the young we are taking a very powerful step to encourage this by setting up institutions where the students are unlikely to be able to live at home, and must therefore be separated from the culture represented by their parents and the society in which they grew up. I think it possible that the role of the new universities in practice, if not in intention, may have been to play a significant part in what history might regard either as the disruption, or the rejuvenation, of our Western European culture.

REFERENCE

NATIONAL UNION OF STUDENTS. 1970. *A Report on the Expansion of Higher Education 1970–80.* London.

The balance between engineering science and practical experience

P. H. CALDERBANK

Engineering is usually understood to be an aspect of the useful application of knowledge or, more specifically, the harnessing of nature to serve man. The laws of nature are relatively few compared to the many combinations of them that may be brought together in devices or systems that serve a useful purpose. It is one purpose of engineers, in their innovative function, to seek out fresh combinations that produce useful systems; another purpose is to study and improve or develop such systems, and yet another to organize the manufacture and operation of these systems in an economical manner.

Most people recognize the importance of engineering in the history of civilization, and in the welfare of this country in particular; furthermore, many people are keenly interested in the products of engineering: they will go far to see new bridges or aeroplanes for example. But despite this, engineering is not a popular subject of study in Britain, it does not attract as high a proportion of the more talented students as does pure science. The reasons for this state of affairs, which is by no means universal, have been often discussed, but inconclusively. I will content myself by pointing to a contributory factor which may be of general interest: this is the inertia that causes systems of education to adapt very slowly to changes in social environment.

We are fortunate in Britain not to have the extreme examples of educational inertia found in some places. Early French systems of education implanted in Iran and Quebec, for example, have preserved in these places unenlightened methods of learning devoted to antique social orders, despite the coexisting desperate social need to make use of abundant natural resources. The Germanic system of higher education in science is inefficient and tedious. In these and similar cases the symptoms are widely known and the cures are identified, but impossible to implement. To a lesser degree the British educational system, although evolving at a discernible rate, still preserves many of the objectives that were appropriate to the administration of a colonial empire, at least in so far as the balance of subject areas is concerned. Why else should this balance be so different in the USA and Russia? In the UK the status and importance of administrative functions seem exaggerated at a time when fewer individual decisions are taken at higher levels; the 'elite' ethos, associated with uncommitted learning, certain professions, and places of learning, at one time an important means of securing respect and discipline, is no longer so relevant, but these are still important factors in the minds of many parents, schoolteachers, and employers.

There is a strong vested interest in preserving the educational status quo. Changes disturb the established order, which depends in many ways on educational selection, sometimes as a kind of initiation rite, this being jealously guarded by individuals and professions with well-developed instincts for self-preservation. These instincts for security and status sometimes lead to 'closed shops' in certain professions, the aim being that the input can be easily adjusted to optimize the professional, as well as the public, wellbeing. Entry to the well-organized professions has become fairly extensively regulated and restricted to university graduates. The engineering profession has so far been an 'open shop', so it lacks the status of an exclusive university input. Attempts to bring about an engineering graduate professional closed shop are in progress at the present time, but this may be only one, rather unattractive, possible late remedy to the problem of recruitment. We find, in contrast, that engineering has enjoyed a high reputation and attracted many able students in universities of the USA and English-speaking Canada, despite the open shop policy. This is almost certainly due first to the early establishment of the 'useful arts' universities such as Cornell and Stanford, founded in protest against the east-coast European-model universities, and second to the foundation of state colleges with obligations of a severely practical kind. Engineering graduates were then used in industry at all levels with great success. This provided the incentive and status for recruitment to the profession so that substitution for engineers by less qualified people was not required on the scale practised in the UK. The point that I am making is that in western universities the balance of subjects available by choice does not faithfully reflect contemporary public need, besides being strongly conservative. While this may be acceptable in an environment subject to slow change, it can be damaging if, as is the case in Britain, society and industry are changing rapidly and higher education is being greatly extended. Will the criteria that guided the choice made by yesterday's few graduates remain sufficient for tomorrow's many? Few can doubt that change will be required, and I think there is at hand an awakening of interest on the part of university students in applied science directed towards social betterment, if only industry will declare an interest in public welfare in the way that it is beginning to in the USA. In my opinion this interest should be stimulated and encouraged because, in the long run, people wish to be involved in the forces that are shaping their lives. Increasingly these forces arise directly from developments in science and engineering, and also indirectly in that developments buy the time to make other things possible. The relationship between higher education and the community is too general a topic and too complex to pursue here, so I shall attempt to define the particular characteristics of engineering education and practice that may be of general interest.

Scientific method has traditionally been ascribed to the ideas of Plato and Bacon, but recent thought suggests that it is not necessary to look for influences outwith those that have shaped the general pattern of civilized ideas. If there is no such thing as a peculiarly scientific method, which I accept to be the case, I am on good ground in claiming that engineering methods are no more distinguishable. It is said that scientists are concerned only with analysis, whereas engineers are also involved with synthesis. In this connection, it is worth noting, however, that technological advance does not necessarily wait for scientific understanding; a phenomenon may be identified and then lead to extensive application long before it is properly understood. For example, we have found, entirely by empirical search, highly specific catalysts for many commercially important chemical reactions. The history of invention is full of other instances where the laws of nature are, in a sense, anticipated.

It is difficult to identify fundamental distinctions between much of the content of university curricula in pure and engineering science, but students emerge from these courses with very different attitudes and objectives, moulded in the image of their teachers. The engineering courses contain two basic elements: a quantitative scientific element covering a broad range; and a body of updated experience. The proportions of these two elements can be widely varied, and the first of them needs no further explanation. The second is the stock-in-trade of the professional practitioner, and is the embodiment of accumulated past experience of trial and improvement in the design, fabrication, and operation of hardware. The engineering science element has a long, useful half-life; the hardware element is subject to continual modification as innovations and developments occur, and part of the store becomes redundant when one device is superseded by another. A pattern is developing in which general engineering science studies occupy more fully the undergraduate curriculum, and specialization is deferred to the latter parts of the course and extended into postgraduate years, while the hardware element, which is only lightly touched on as exemplification or in design exercises, is increasingly left to become a part of training and experience in industry.

The temptation to ask too much from the student is strong. We are fortunate at the University of Edinburgh in that engineering science was able to adopt the very general science faculty regulations, and thus ensure that our demand on students keeps in step with the consensus of opinion as to what is reasonable as regards both the breadth of course and the work-load. There will always be some concern with training for professional competence; this does not simply mean that all important topics be read and understood but, in addition, that sufficient practice must be given to ensure reliability in design calculations over the whole spread of student ability. This is an area where laboratory work has declined in favour of tutorial and design classes – with some sacrifice, not the least of which is a too ready tendency to adopt conventional solutions in cases where experiment and innovation would be more desirable.

I think I have said enough to justify the conclusion that there are severe problems of how to balance engineering education, and the decisions reached as to the balance desired in any given institution result from a complex combination of influences which, altering in importance with time as they do, should exercise an adaptive control on subsequent necessary change, if a flexible structure of courses and regulations is provided.

I now wish to point to the unresolved problem of the optimum environment for engineering education. I think that there is evidence that governments wish to promote engineering education particularly for obvious economic reasons, and it is not always satisfactory to allow this to take place through a university community who do not share the same sense of priority. Hence the technological universities and, more recently, the polytechnics are promoted as channels for the more specific direction of funds. I think it is unlikely that universities in general will remain forever immune to analogous pressures, also arising from the laws of employment supply and demand. Will it continue to be accepted that any academic endeavour is a preparation for living, and will it become known that preparations for living and working are not mutually exclusive? Students must continue to follow their interests and talents, but these are themselves some function of the educational system, and with many more graduates competing for jobs and a more centralized and professional management of affairs, it seems likely that the arts and leisure industries will formulate more professional criteria of the kind already found in journalism, drama, graphic art, etc.

Engineering is sometimes called a useful art and I have entirely neglected any reference to this aspect of it, yet it is that feature that, for many, elevates an expertise into an absorbing preoccupation. The design of artefacts and systems allows of many solutions of varying fitness and appeal; the finished result departs from perfection but even a modest degree of success has personality and satisfaction for those who have conspired at it. I have already referred to the open shop character of engineering practice; a limited knowledge still allows one to practise in a limited field and originality of thought is at a premium. Even more important is the enthusiasm and perseverance required to develop a concept to a successful hardware conclusion. The process of prototype trial and modification known as development is necessary because engineering is the art of compromise. The effort and cost of development has often been commented upon, and one aim of engineering science is to reduce these elements by reducing the uncertainty of design; while this remains, the only remedies will be intuition and experience.

These two qualities conflict to some extent; ingenuity must not be allowed to extend too far into novelty, while past experience cannot be wholly relied upon. Progress, with an acceptable risk, is sought. The many parts of a development project interact so that a decision on one aspect affects later decisions and other aspects of the programme. To return to an earlier theme, engineering is like living, a cooperative endeavour leading to change that is dependent on past decisions. Joint enterprises encourage the development of specialized individual proficiency, and while this is valuable when the enterprises remain broadly similar in kind, experts do not readily change their fields at the rate required. The rate of change of technology is easily exaggerated; in general there is a relatively slow process of steady improvement in hardware aimed at reliability, performance, and low cost, although the accompanying impact on society may take place rapidly. On rare occasions a breakthrough occurs, and this calls for exceptional adaptability on the part of those engineers who participate; others may find their expertise becoming obsolete, as changes act with greatest intensity at their source.

It is interesting to observe that in some, so-called, 'backward' eastern civilizations how ancient mechanical skills are preserved at a high level in the arts and crafts, and how readily these skills can be deployed for the maintenance of advanced mechanical equipment. This is, however, skill in reproduction and should not be confused with engineering, which is devoted to the art of change.

SUMMARY

Engineers try to create systems of hardware that change the constraints on man's experience. Systems of higher education reflect, but lag behind, the needs of society, which tends to resist educational change to a remarkable degree.

It seems reasonable to expect a natural expansion in engineering education in this country when the purposes and character of engineering become more widely appreciated. Engineering demands creative talent as well as scientific knowledge and practical experience in varying proportions; this has resulted in many different avenues of admission into the profession, and requires adaptability from the practitioner when the proportions alter due to technological change.

Engineering education is likely to become a series of postgraduate training courses founded on broad-based undergraduate curricula containing pure and engineering science. Engineering science is concerned with the behaviour of systems in which natural laws interact in ways that are usually too complex to allow rigorous analytical solution, while engineering training is a body of correlated observation and experience exemplified by case studies and design exercises.

© P. H. Calderbank 1973

The psychological basis of subject-choice

LIAM HUDSON

The universities have survived for centuries without making any systematic examination of their own endeavour. Now that such a process of self-examination has begun, certain among us, the psychologists and social scientists especially perhaps, find ourselves embarrassed. Figures in authority, rather than leaving us to plough our lonely furrows, have begun to question us about the shape our institutions should have. We are called abruptly from our pursuits in a corner of the academic garden and required to apply ourselves, in the role of expert, to the problems the real world presents. If we retain even the residual glimmering of honesty that a life of committee work permits, we will know that we don't know; that, in the world of practical affairs, the academic expert is in truth little better off than his neighbour. Our first impulse, one I hope we stifle, is to bluff: to wrap up our hunches in a bundle of technical language, to quote statistics, and to trust that we are taken on trust.

In the event, though, relevant knowledge is hard to come by, and the better informed you are, the sharper your wits, the sparser you find it to be. There is, admittedly, a certain amount of knowledge on the periphery of the social and behavioural sciences that, at the first glance, looks as though it is relevant. This is the fruit of applied research, funded usually because it struck a busy civil servant as looking down to earth rather than airy-fairy or because someone somewhere had a problem to solve, and needed to back his prejudice in the matter with some seemingly appropriate facts and figures. Such research enjoys low professional esteem, partly for snobbish reasons, partly because it is usually intellectually unsubstantial, and partly because it is so often undertaken cynically, as a way of raising funds. The professional response so far has been to retreat to issues of greater elegance and no practical value. My contention is that this polarity, between the sham useful and the genuinely useless, though it appears natural and at times inevitable, is not one that we should mutely accept. I would like to envisage educational research that is relevant without being menial, that not merely collects facts, though these are scarce enough in all conscience, but also illuminates the beliefs about human nature and human institutions that lend meaning to facts.

Instead of reviewing a large but mostly barren literature, I would like to present three pieces of evidence, one recent, the other two still in the making. I have chosen them because they interest me, because they bear on the question of subject-choice in a new and perhaps illuminating way, because they may succeed in embroiling the reader for a moment or two in the doubts and uncertainties of psychological argument, and, most important of all, because they fail to conform to current prejudices about usefulness in research. If this work is relevant to practicalities, it is so for reasons more persuasive than superficial appearance suggests. Our task is to select problems that matter, to collect evidence that is relevant rather than merely seeming so, and to explore and refine the systems of meaning in which both problems and evidence reside.

It is a good working rule in the kind of research I do that to find out something new about the relation of individuals to institutions, you look at those areas that the institution itself defines informally as vaguely bogus. (It has dawned on me only slowly that institutions use informal systems of taboo to protect themselves from prying eyes.) The three pieces of evidence I now wish to place before you meet this requirement admirably: each has about it just this telltale air of illegitimacy. On the surface, they appear entirely unrelated. My plan is to show that interconnections exist nonetheless, and to use these interconnections as the basis for some more general remarks about academic subjects and the balance between them. And I want to do this, quite self-consciously, not as an exercise in logically binding inference – something quite unrealistic in the present state of the art – but as an exercise in interpretation.

It is obvious that academic specialists differ, intellectually, of course, but also in personality and temperament. The electrical engineer is a different kind of person from the consultant physician, from the psychologist, from the littérateur. Such distinctions are often quite finely drawn. Electrical engineers, for example, are sometimes held to differ, both intellectually and temperamentally, from mechanical engineers. Physicists, likewise, conventionally distinguish between theoretical specialists and experimental specialists. Physicians are often taken to differ from surgeons, and surgeons from, say, anatomists. In my own trade, the harder, more scientific psychologists seem to be separable in a number of ways from the softer and more humane ones. This phenomenon has intrigued me since I started research, and it is of practical significance, because if academic specialists differ, and if the balance between subjects alters, then the balance between the types of person a university produces alters accordingly. Each of the pieces of research I shall mention springs from this interest in academic differences. Superficially, the directions in which they seem to spring are entirely disparate. I maintain, however, that they bear on one another in an illuminating and unexpected way.

The first example concerns the question of professional image or stereotype. I started this work in 1966 and finished it in 1968 (see Hudson 1967a, 1967b, also Hudson 1968). At that time, as is still the case, professional stereotypes were felt to be vaguely disreputable, the preserve of the advertising industry. Broadly my findings, in conjunction with American work, suggested that schoolboys envisage the various academic professions in spectral terms, with the artist and the physical scientist positioned one at each end of the spectrum. The physical scientist, the mathematician, and the engineer are all seen as hard; the artist, novelist, and poet as soft. The physical scientist is seen as intelligent, manly, cold, dependable, and valuable; the artist as imaginative, rather feminine, warm, undependable, and relatively worthless. The artist is seen as sexually active, the scientist as sexually inert. Technically, there are a variety of tunes that one can play on data like these. Only one concerns us here: the curious fact that while schoolboys from the age of eleven onwards, and irrespective of their career intentions, agree about the image of the scientist, that of the artist crystallizes only gradually in the course of adolescence.

So, fact number one: the scientist is seen from an early age as hard, cold, and valuable, certainly from before the onset both of adolescence and of academic specialization; the artist is seen as soft, warm, and worthless – but this consensus takes shape only later. In isolation, this fact makes no sense at all. There are, however, two further pieces of evidence to set beside it. First, the fact that scientific interests, like musical ones, often show themselves among the very young, in the earliest years of primary schooling, or even before. Second, the fact that among secondary schoolboys, those specializing in science seem to commit themselves academically at a younger age than do those specializing in the arts.

Now, for some years, I have worked with the distinction between convergers and divergers, between convergent and divergent forms of intelligence. The converger is the person with a marked bias of ability towards the analytic types of intelligence tested by the conventional IQ test; the diverger is the person with a bias towards the more fluent, more intuitive, less rational forms of thinking encouraged by open-ended tasks – like thinking of uses for everyday objects. If I may summarize a great deal in a sentence or two, I have found, and others seem to have confirmed, that when academic specialization offers a choice between courses that are more analytic on the one hand, and more intuitive and humane on the other, convergers tend, not surprisingly, to go into the first, divergers into the second. Biological science, incidentally, seems to attract convergers and divergers in roughly equal proportions. It is also clear that convergers and divergers differ temperamentally, divergers being the more willing to express the personal and non-rational aspects of their mental lives, convergers being more controlled and more conventional. The converger–scientist, then, is in some sense more inhibited than the diverger–arts specialist. But this inhibition, rather than being an integral part of who he is, may only manifest itself in a reluctance to answer questions that seem to him foolish. There is a great deal of circumstantial evidence about mature scientists to suggest that this difference is, in fact, an integral one, but no evidence, as far as I know, that bears on this point directly. It was for this reason that another eminently dubious topic was broached: the question of whether convergers find it as easy as divergers to recall their dreams. Mark Austin, a research student in my department, has taken this on (Austin 1971). He has subjected small groups of convergent and divergent undergraduates to the rigours of the sleep laboratory. The study is neat, and the result unequivocal. Convergers, while appearing, physiologically speaking, to have the same number of dreams as divergers – that is to say, they exhibit roughly the same amounts of 'rapid eye-movement' sleep – are much less likely to recall their dreams when wakened from them.

They are also less likely to report dreams involving people or aggression. Austin's study suggests, in other words, that differences between the converger–scientist and the diverger–arts specialist reflect deep-seated rather than superficial aspects of psychic life. So far, then, we have stereotypes of the arts and the sciences, and dream recall. The third piece of evidence arose from efforts on my own part to be down to earth and operational about certain ideas – personality and temperament – that psychologists usually treat in rather artificial terms; to look at the lives people lead, and in particular at their patterns of marriage and fertility. In practice, this has meant reading that curious document *Who's Who* from cover to cover, looking to see whether schoolboys' images of the typical arts specialist and the typical physical scientist are in any literal sense true (Hudson and Jacot 1971).

The data from *Who's Who* have turned out to be unexpectedly rich: hares, red herrings, white elephants have started in all directions. Again, I shall be highly selective. If you look at eminent arts specialists, and biological and physical scientists, born between 1900 and 1925, and educated in this country, you find that they differ in their tendency to remain single, in the age at which they marry, in the frequency with which they have childless marriages, and in their tendency to divorce. Scholars in the arts (classics, philosophy, history, English literature) tend to an unexpected degree to remain single, or to have childless marriages. Over 40 per cent, for example, of the classicists had no children. They also were quite likely to marry late, after the age of thirty-five, but, with the exception of the philosophers, they were unlikely to be divorced. In contrast, almost all the eminent scientists marry. The biological scientists are the more likely to marry late, to have large families, and to be divorced. The physical scientists – chemists, metallurgists, academic engineers, geologists, physicists – follow a more conventional pattern: few late marriages, medium-sized families, and very low rates of divorce. (The physicists, we may note in passing, are aberrant in this last respect, being relatively susceptible to divorce. Mathematicians seem to fall quite outside the physical science pattern, belonging most nearly with the arts specialists.) Other groups were also studied: social scientists, who are distinguished by a high divorce rate; creative writers, who seem to be single, married, and divorced in almost equal proportions; and medical specialists, of whom more in a moment.

Next comes the task of considering these three elements in relation to one another. My aim, as I have already said, is not to tie them into a logically coherent theory with postulates and predictions, but simply to make some psychological sense and suggest where we might profitably look next. The three elements seem in fact to cohere around a very simple, if unfashionable, developmental model, one that hinges broadly on the distinction between three developmental stages, infancy, childhood, and adolescence; on the distinction between the rational and the non-rational; and on the notion of personal identity – our sense of who we are, and what befits us. I do not intend that this be a detailed exposition, merely a sketch.

Whatever their theoretical persuasions, psychologists who deal with children assume an evolution from an infantile state of preoccupation with bodily sensations, to some form of working relationship with the external world. This process is known to psychoanalysts as 'reality testing', and is usually held to be well under way by the age of five. From then until the onset of puberty, the child has been said to enter a 'latency period', one in which his primary concerns are not so much with his own bodily needs, as with learning the elementary skills – reading, writing, calculating – and with making sense of his environment. This period of impersonal exploration is assumed to last until the massive hormonal changes that occur in the early teens and herald sexual maturity. The latency period may thus be characterized as a phase in which children explore their rational capabilities; adolescence as one in which they are confronted, once again, with the non-rational.

The evidence about the stereotypes of arts and science now begins to make a little sense. The stereotype of the scientist evolves in children's minds at a time when they are concerned to control the irrational aspects of their own natures; and it epitomizes the qualities that such internal control demands. The scientist is seen as valuable, hard, but cold. The stereotype of the artist emerges later, when adolescents are beginning to grapple with life's more personal, more emotional, more erotic potentialities. The artist is seen as soft, warm, but as lacking in value. Arguably, too, the identities of convergent and divergent children can be seen as crystallizing at different stages: the convergent during the latency period, the divergent in adolescence. The internal economy of the convergent child, the future scientist, might be said to gel at the stage in his development when issues of rationality and internal control are paramount. That of the divergent child, the future arts specialist, becomes fixed at a stage when emotional considerations are more pressing. And on this argument, one would predict that the diverger's experience of adolescence is more turbulent than that of convergers, that he is less capable of pursuing impersonal argument for its own sake, and that he has readier access to his own intuitions, fantasies, dreams. Austin's research certainly fits into this pattern. In broad outline, the work on marriage and fertility does so too; the conventional patterns of personal life being found among the physical scientists, the less conventional among the biologists, social scientists, and arts specialists.

Obviously, I have been paraphrasing brutally here. People do not divide simply into the convergent and divergent; the academic world does not divide simply into the arts and sciences. And even when such a model is given due elaboration, there are differences – for instance, that between the marital behaviour of arts scholars and creative writers, between physicists and chemists – that it cannot yet encompass. An occupational hazard among psychologists is that of offering reductive explanations: of describing vastly complex ecological processes entirely in terms of single organisms and their internal states. War is reduced to aggression, student militance to rivalry with the father, painting to faecal play. I shall try to avoid this preemptive heresy, and to do so by going back to my data, specifically to two more outgrowths of the work on *Who's Who*.

First, let me take you back to the divorce rate among eminent biologists. This stands at a little over 12 per cent, and, compared with the rates among other scientists, is high. The oddity of this finding is that nearly all the divorces in question come from a small subset of the biologists: those born in the first decade of the century, and educated at public schools. Among this group, the rate of divorce is approximately one in five; and, again, standing alone, this datum is inexplicable, but, happily, one is not totally adrift. Looking for other groups with high divorce rates, one finds the social scientists and the creative writers; also, though much more modestly, the philosophers and the physicists. The physicists have not yet yielded up a clear pattern, but the philosophers have: those who divorce tend to have been born in the second decade of the century, not the first. In detail, they are for the most part those associated with the positivistic revolution in British philosophy that took place in the

1930s and 1940s, and was centred on Oxford. Fancifully perhaps, one senses firm ground beneath one's feet once more, if the history of science can be described in such robust terms. One recalls Thomas Kuhn's distinction between the revolutionary and normal phases in the development of a science, and his warning that the qualities that suit an individual to one may not suit him to the other (Kuhn 1970). A body of knowledge may need divergers in times of upheaval, convergers at times of more normal growth. It seems to me possible that those who gain eminence in the formative stages of their discipline's growth may be more divergent, and hence more divorce prone, than those whose eminence is achieved in more stable times. I am less than confident about the application of this explanation to biology, but it is consistent with what I know of the recent history of philosophy, and with that of the social sciences, where revolution is more or less continuous.

From the psychology of human development we have moved to the history of science and the sociology of knowledge. My second example follows a rather similar course. In a parallel study using *Who's Who* we have looked at eminent members of the medical profession, the role models at whom medical students gaze in admiration. Here our analysis was primarily in terms of educational background: whether the specialists in question had gone to a public or grammar school, to a school in England, as opposed to one in Scotland, Wales, or Northern Ireland (Hudson & Jacot, in preparation). We found that on the whole, those doctors who exercise clinical authority over patients, i.e. surgeons and physicians, were more likely to have been to an English public school than those whose contact with patients is less direct – anatomists, physiologists, pharmacologists, and so on. Among surgeons, a further categorization is possible: in terms of the part of the body on which they operate. Those who worked exclusively on the head (ear, nose and throat, ophthalmic) were more likely to have gone to English public schools than those who work below the waist (gastro-intestinal and rectal, urological, obstetric, gynaecological). Further distinctions can be drawn between specialists who work on living bodies, as opposed to dead bodies or parts of bodies; on male bodies, as opposed to female bodies; on the surface of the body, as opposed to its insides. In each case, the first group of specialists is more likely to come from an English public school than is the second. Scottish public and direct grant schools, in contrast, produce more than their share of psychiatrists; English grammar schools a preponderance of dentists, anaesthetists, and pharmacologists.

Though statistically robust, and at least mildly amusing, these findings make no sense unless one is prepared to argue in social, even perhaps anthropological, terms. I am reminded, for example, of the point made by the anthropologist Mary Douglas (1966) that low status and defilement are structurally linked. Whatever the correct explanation, the example does suggest how subtle are the forces that act on a student when he is trying to match his abilities and predispositions to a professional identity.

I hope that these points have not confused you but perhaps have persuaded you that a student's choice of subject may reflect preferences that are themselves rooted in his earlier life and upbringing; that intellectual and personal matters are not sharply differentiated, except perhaps in the lives of those individuals whose internal economy demands that this should be so; that, as subjects of study, the intellectual and the personal cannot usefully be separated. We do not confront organisms with black boxes in their crania, but coherent organisms in which the intellectual and personal are related in lawful if inscrutable ways. But we are just beginning, still scratching at the surface of a topic as complex as any in science, and for the most part using conceptual distinctions that advance very little on common sense. On the strength of even these humble beginnings, nonetheless, one can begin to identify areas of special concern.

First, and most obviously, factual inadequacies. We know incredibly little, for example, about the development of interests in children and young adolescents; we know almost nothing about the latency period, we are not even sure whether it is really latent; and we know nothing yet about the forces in a child's background that encourage him to lock on to one set of pursuits, or to delay, to defer commitment. Again, there is little research of any quality on the lives academic specialists lead: how they work, who they work with, how they compartmentalize their time, who they marry, how they marry, how they deploy their loyalties and their affections.

There are questions, too, of more immediate educational relevance. We know little about the processes whereby a student acquires the traditions and the style of thought pertaining to a particular academic discipline, nor do we know, once he has acquired these, under what circumstances they serve in practice as a cultural barrier, cutting him off from many, sometimes nearly all, of his academic colleagues. Nor are we aware of what happens when, for whatever reason, we try to push people against the grain of their natural inclination: what happens when we try to introduce a history student, let us say, to the field of statistics or a geneticist to sociological rather than biological modes of explanation. Sometimes the obstacles seem to be those of competence, at other times matters of primitive loyalty and fear of the alien and unknown.

It is obvious that one cannot proceed in an economic, cultural, or political vacuum. Constraints external to the university may require that we push people against the grain in large and perhaps increasing numbers, by making them work in ways they find subtly antipathetic. The demand for graduates who are numerically and technologically competent may well continue to increase, likewise the demand for technologists who are culturally and also perhaps morally alert. Pedagogically, the prospect is daunting. University teaching has evolved, to a considerable extent, as a process whereby one like-minded person teaches another. The set of techniques and rituals that has resulted may well be unsuited to occasions when minds are not alike, where there are cultural barriers and primitive fears to be overcome. Transdisciplinary teaching is at the moment a matter for brave and lonely experiment. I hope that we will soon proceed more systematically, and that we will do so, not in a series of fashionable lunges, but more circumspectly, taking note as we go.

The problem of evaluating educational innovations, especially in terms of their longer-term influence on students, is one that will not be solved quickly, and perhaps never with elegance. The idea that the universities are willing to innovate, and willing, too, to look systematically at the consequences, is from my own point of view welcome. The benefit to the psychologists and social scientists concerned will be unambiguous. We will be able to base our thinking about the growth of intelligence not on the artificial and circumstantial, but on evidence of what real brain-work consists in. The possible benefits for the university are more speculative, I concede. But people like myself, if we bend ourselves to the task, may be able to construe what is going on in the minds of students in a way that the isolated teacher cannot. Knowledge of the consequences of our actions is not invariably destructive, either of our aplomb, or of the stability of our institutions. There is a case for blind faith, certainly, but also one for faith tempered with a modicum of information. The process whereby an institution renders itself explicable is nonetheless a complex one, and full of awkward surprises. Many of its processes, like those of its individual members, are non-rational; questions, for instance, of trust, loyalty, identification. To render itself transparent both to its own members and to society at large may be a perilous endeavour, and not one to be undertaken lightly, nor dashed at in any crudely scientistic fashion. I think, and hope, that we are now committed to making the attempt. Even so, we must be prepared, I think, to make blunders and recoup them; and to preserve, at least residually, our appreciation of the mythical, phantasmagoric, and bizarre. I hope, in other words, that our efforts will be imbued with precisely the values that are implicit in this account of intellectual development, namely that we will be both intelligent and imaginative; that we will allow space to the non-rational as well as to the rational; and that we will preserve the sense of identity – intangible but potent – on which the life of an institution, as of an individual, may eventually prove to depend.

REFERENCES

AUSTIN, M. 1971. Dream Recall and the Bias of Intellectual Ability. *Nature.*

DOUGLAS, M. 1966. *Purity and Danger.* London: Routledge and Kegan Paul.

KUHN, T. 1970. The Essential Tension, Tradition and Innovation in Scientific Research. In L. Hudson (ed.), *The Ecology of Human Intelligence.* Harmondsworth: Penguin.

HUDSON, L. 1967a. The Stereotypical Scientist. *Nature.*

HUDSON, L. 1967b. Arts and Sciences: The Influence of Stereotypes on Language. *Nature.*

HUDSON, L. 1968. *Frames of Mind.* London: Methuen.

HUDSON, L. and JACOT, B. 1971. Marriage and Fertility in Academic Life. *Nature.*

HUDSON, L., and JACOT, B. 1971. Education and Eminence in British Medicine. *British Medical Journal.*

Sixteen to twenty-one: the 'debatable area'

ROGER YOUNG

A Glasgow publisher launched a new series of guides in 1970 on aspects of tertiary education, tertiary being regarded as 'the debatable area that lies after school, whether defined as further or higher education'. The phrase caught my eye and provided me with the title for this essay. Ironically, however, the series itself is not engaging in a debate about this area at all. Perhaps we should not be surprised. There has been little suggestion that a radical debate is needed about the *structure* of education for those above the age of sixteen. While scrutiny of costs, projections of statistics, discussion about the nature and function of the constituent parts of the structure, taken individually, have been undertaken there has been no debate about the system as such. There appears to be a general assumption that at the least it should remain the unsystematic jumble it is – sixth-form colleges; further education colleges; colleges of education, of technology, and of commerce; university colleges, and even, for part of the lower end of the age-range, Cheltenham College, Winchester College, and George Watson's College. It is like a jigsaw puzzle where the wrong pieces have been fitted together, not only leaving gaps here and overlaps there, but failing to produce what a jigsaw is supposed to produce when completed – an intelligible picture. How unintelligible the picture actually is only becomes evident when one attempts to explain it to the hopeful visiting American, African, or Russian.

Open and wide-ranging debate, therefore, about this area of education does seem to be called for. Nor am I too apologetic about rushing in where academic, civil service, and political angels fear to tread. Perhaps only a fool would ask whether we have got the

pattern of post-sixteen-year-old education right, and only a rash
fool would suggest he had a better one. If so, I am probably as well
qualified as any to do both these things. The debate must start
somewhere and the sooner the better.

First, it may be of interest to recall some of the varied factors that
led me to these considerations. One was a set of questions sent to
universities in 1969 which asked for views on a number of possible
ways of reducing unit-costs per student in the next ten years, during
which time student numbers seemed likely to double again. Another
was the publication of the Schools' Council's proposal in England
for Q and F examinations to replace A levels. Had the proposals any
merit? Had they any relevance to Scotland? A third factor was a
comment made to me by a professor of geology in the Royal School
of Mines, at Imperial College, London, to the effect that their
students were very good specialists, but hadn't enough time to
absorb and develop non-specialist interests and skills. A fourth was
my personal frustration at the eternal wrangle between Scots and
English enthusiasts for their own tradition in education – a wrangle
consisting of odious and almost entirely irrelevant comparisons.

These starting-points suggested to me the urgent need to rethink
our whole pattern of secondary and higher education, and so this is
the basic theme of this paper. I believe that we have a large number
of important problems facing us which are being tackled separately
instead of together. Every solution to a problem that is dealt with in
isolation from the others leads to more difficulties being created
elsewhere. There seems no end to this process of putting new strains
on other parts of the system by solving a problem in one part. Hence
my plea for an attempt to look at the system as a whole.

I shall begin by indicating some of these issues in a series of
questions, starting at the lower end of the age-group.

Are we satisfied with a situation in which, compared with other
developed countries, Britain has virtually the lowest rates of staying
on in fulltime education after the age of sixteen and seventeen?
When Americans, in particular, express their surprise about this, one
naturally explains about the Industrial Training Act and all the
other excellent things done parttime by sixteen-, seventeen-, and
eighteen-year-olds. But I do not think that this is good enough.

Are General Certificate of Education A levels working to our
satisfaction? To judge by the almost continuous, if vain, attempts on
the part of the English to find alternatives over the last fifteen years,

I imagine the answer must be no. They have put forward I levels, F levels, Q levels, subsidiary levels, modular credit systems, and so on, only to reject each in turn. This implies that more than just A levels have gone wrong.

Similar doubts strike me about the philosophy of the Scottish sixth-year certificate: its division and subdivision into smaller and more specialized subjects do not imply a healthy respect for wider educational aims, rather they suggest a scramble for power, through examinations, on the part of specialists for whom their own subject is the only important, if not the only, pebble on the beach.

Questions about GCE and Scottish Certificate of Education lead to two further sets of questions. First, those that concern the provision of teaching resources for these examinations: do we really think the present kaleidoscopic patterns of secondary education (particularly the duplication of certificate work in schools and further education colleges) are desirable or economically viable? And can they be matched by adequate teaching resources for our fifth and sixth forms? The projected shortage of 800 mathematics teachers in Scotland in 1976 does not make for optimism. Nor does the 1968 study by the Inner London Education Authority on *sixth-form opportunities*, which revealed the serious difficulties in staffing that faces the ILEA in the 1970s if it goes ahead with a universal policy of comprehensive schools for eleven- to eighteen-year-olds. I fancy the situation is not all that different in, say, Aberdeen. How will that city really provide the full range of courses in the sixth-form year of the ten comprehensive schools spread so neatly round the city? How will it find the specialist teachers to look after them? The answer is, I believe, that it will not and cannot. As the Public Schools Commission shows, the size of the sixth-form year in a comprehensive school of even 1,300 pupils is so small as to make the prospect of doing this utopian. Even a full range of fifth-form courses will be difficult to staff in all schools. And Aberdeen is an affluent area when it comes to staffing, so heaven help Lanarkshire!

Second, what about university selection? Are A levels and highers (SCE) suitable instruments for this, let alone the best? I do not pretend to know, though discussion of failure rates at least suggests that the question is worth asking. Indeed, if they are not particularly good selective instruments now, how much less will they serve the needs of more competitive conditions in five to ten years' time.

Again, are we really convinced that very large schools of 1,500 pupils and over from 11 or 12 to 18 are the ideal form of school community for all? The management problems are not yet fully appreciated, nor are the effects on the pupils who attend such institutions. We must take care that the economies in staffing that increased size can produce are not lost by multiplying supportive, advisory, pastoral, and other non-teaching staff. But unless we are sensitive about the need for such staff to offset the weight of administrative problems and the impersonality of a very big school, we shall fail to make the school a real community and thus have an even more serious social problem on our hands. The experience of New York schools and other huge American high schools provides enough evidence to warn us against thinking any easy solution to this paradox can be found.

In any case, do we really think that in the next thirty years pupils of 17, 18, and 19 will willingly go on attending 'schools', in the sense in which we use that term now? What about their changing social, personal, and organizational needs? The increasing maturity of these young people and the fact of far larger numbers staying on in fulltime education beyond the age of 16 and 17 will transform the style of their education in such a way that 'schools' are no longer likely to be the appropriate place for them. For I see this group as increasingly restive (and there is plenty of evidence for this, particularly in the south) if kept within a school's bounds and atmosphere. Similarly, the 15 to 16 age-group increasingly needs responsibility and status within the school community. They are unlikely to get either when the 17 to 18 age-group is still 'on top' of them.

There is one more major problem that must be mentioned, and while it may be unpopular to suggest that this is worth examination, we cannot afford socially and economically to go on ignoring it indefinitely. I refer to the increasing importance of parental, and therefore, of course, of pupil, mobility in our educational planning. Promotion for large numbers of people now depends on a willingness to move readily – and, in many cases, frequently – from area to area, and from one education authority to another. It is a tragic paradox for these families that in a period of increasing population mobility we have made it more rather than less difficult for children to change schools. For, as responsible parents soon discover, a change of school almost always also involves a change of systems. How much longer will they have to put up with the present frustrating differences between, for example, the English and Scottish patterns of education? Indeed, why should they be expected to? How much longer can heads of schools and their staffs be expected to go on wasting valuable time acclimatizing children to the changes they face when crossing the border in either direction, or indeed when crossing education authority boundaries? How much longer can we ask children who change schools to pay a heavy price to uphold national traditions in England and Scotland – traditions supposedly maintained for the sake of the very pupils who suffer from them?

I must turn now to some problems that are closer to the central theme of this volume, but nevertheless cannot, I believe, be dealt with independently of the problems that I have just been discussing. The most threatening of all, I suppose, are those concerning numbers and finance. How are we going, not just to meet, but to plan effectively, constructively, and appropriately for the doubling of qualified entrants into higher education in the next ten years? And how are we going to do it economically, in the sense of getting the best value for our public and private money? Some suggestions for easing the difficulties were put forward in 1969 by the then Minister of State. The difficulty about the thirteen possible lines of action was not so much that university people could and did think of serious objections to every one of them, but that, even if no one had objected to any, the main problem of costs still would not have been solved. Least of all would any coherent pattern or policy for the fundamental structure of higher education have emerged from their adoption. Nor is there any positive help to be found in the 1970 memoranda from the Scottish Education Department and the Department of Education and Science on student numbers in higher education. These memoranda have been widely criticized by many experts. As an amateur, I should like merely to emphasize the point made by most of them: that the memoranda claim to be based on 'neutral' assumptions, whereas in fact no assumptions in this field can be neutral. Professor Vaizey's paper (pp. 171–83) brings out a number of the fallacies that arise from this so-called neutral stance of the Departments. Tyrell Burgess (1970) is even more scathing about it; because of their alleged neutral assumptions about numbers and social change the documents are, he says, 'quite useless as an aid to policy-making' on 'what higher education might be like in 1980'. The *Times Educational Supplement* for Scotland goes further still in its criticism of the Scottish memorandum, for it suggests that in the guise of projections on 'steadystate' assumptions, the SED has in fact foisted on us hidden policies and decisions unawares.

In my view there are two other major sets of questions to be asked before we can assume that the structure of higher education should continue approximately in its present form (that is apart from looking after twice the number of students at much less than twice the cost!).

To begin with, are we satisfied with the present combination – or lack of it – of specialized and general education? If not (and most people would say we are not), how can we combine study in depth with postponement of specialization from an early age? How can we achieve the desirably broad secondary education that everyone says he wants? Within the present structures and assumptions I think the answer is that we cannot. That is probably why the suggestions put forward in the last fifteen years have either failed or not been taken up. Adequate answers are therefore going to involve radical changes in the structures themselves, and these, it will be said, will cost money. Yes, they will; but that is not the real issue. Accommodating double our present numbers in higher education as it is structured today will also cost money. The proper question is therefore whether the latter is in fact the best way to spend it, thus leaving all the educational questions unanswered; or whether it is not worth trying to solve the educational questions at the same time as dealing with the massive increase in numbers. In particular it must be remembered that the increases envisaged in the next ten years do not take us to the end of the road. Expansion will continue thereafter, and if the present framework is creaking under present stresses, how much longer will it stand the strain under future pressure? Is not this the time, then, to think about a new framework and plan it to meet the rising demands, not just of the next ten years, but of the next thirty years. One only needs to look at the rapidity of change in secondary structures in the last twenty-five years to realize that it is the structure of higher education thirty years hence that we must be thinking about now. This leads directly to the other major question I wish to pose: if we have that rather longer time-scale in mind, does the binary system really make sense?

In 1945 the brave new educational world of the Butler Act created in principle a tripartite system of secondary education that was rational and coherent, and appeared to be practicable. In practice it turned out to be a binary system, and one that within ten years was under heavy fire; within twenty years it was more or less in ruins; and within thirty years of the 1944 Acts it will be little more than an unpleasant memory. Why did this happen? Because the 1944 Acts were so rational that they ignored the psychology of human reactions. In the not-so-long run neither parents nor pupils were prepared to be selected out of one part of the system and dumped into the other.

In the light of this experience I for one am far from happy about setting up a pattern in tertiary education that is based on a similar separation of institutions into two parallel sectors of unequal status and prestige. However unfair this may be to individual institutions, this is how the binary pattern will increasingly be viewed by those who aspire to higher education. And the greater the pressure on available places, the greater the gap in status and prestige that will be created in the minds of the applicants. Why should we expect it to be otherwise?

I have asked more than enough questions. Can any answers to them be found? One thing is certain: they cannot be dealt with piecemeal. No doubt it would be too much to expect them all to disappear by presenting one solution, but at least we must aim to look at them together, with a view to devising a quite new post-sixteen-year-old structure. To be worth serious consideration the new pattern will, in my view, have to come as close as possible to satisfying the conditions given below, and since our present structures satisfy none of them the search for one that might even satisfy several of them would be well worth while.

1 We need more time. A great many of our problems arise from the fact that we are vainly attempting in Britain to put a quart into a pint pot. We must accept a longer 'span' of education.

2 The English and Scottish systems of education should be unified, *not* in the sense of one swallowing up the other but in the sense of creating a *new* system common to both countries. Whatever the glories of either in the past, the present barriers between the two systems created by their differences will be intolerable in the 1970s and 1980s.

3 Expansion of educational opportunity is not necessarily best achieved by mere expansion in size. It would be wise to recognize that secondary schools above a certain size – usually rather smaller than our educational planners like to suppose – are subject to serious and dangerous problems, problems that we

are not likely to overcome successfully, at least not on a national scale. The same applies to universities and other institutions of higher education, though the range of size is quite different here from the range that is likely to operate successfully in secondary schools.

4 Educational institutions should not be put in parallel if they are not in practice going to have parity of esteem. Variety of choice should not be mixed up with invidious status distinctions that are generated by the very nature of the institutions.

5 The pressurized, 'rat-race' characteristic of our present system must be removed as far as possible. This does not mean eliminating examinations, or academic 'hurdles', or the necessity for forming judgements about people's capacity to undertake certain kinds of work. It means removing the arbitrary element in our present system which sets certain levels of achievement as a requirement for going on to the next stage of education, and then rejects a sizable proportion of those who meet those requirements.

6 The system should provide opportunities for general education no less than for commercial, vocational, and specialized academic education. As Principal Drever of Dundee University pointed out recently (1970) in a speech that quoted from the Royal Commission of 1826, the provision of higher education should 'enable relatively large numbers of people to get . . . that knowledge which tends to liberalise and make intelligent the mass of our population'. Professor Drever goes on to say that we need to avoid a 'plague of unemployed specialist graduates. . . . These will have thought they were qualifying to enter a particular occupation which in the event did not need them'. In this situation the fact that 'graduates are not qualified for any profession in particular becomes an advantage'.

7 What we commonly understand in Britain by the idea of the university should not be devalued. A comprehensive university might or might not be an admirable thing, but it could no longer be a university as the British have traditionally understood the term. In any case, I am sure that an ever-increasing university entry, with an ever-increasing first-year failure rate to compensate for the difficulty of selection, is not a constructive way to deal with the demand for more higher education. Nor do I think that the parallel provision of academic and non-academic courses, as suggested by Professor Kemmer, is really the right or the most

economic way of solving the problem. Nor is its counterpart – academic, less academic, and non-academic universities – an appropriate solution. By and large this is what America has done, and in such a way that the value of a degree is judged by the ranking of the institution that awards it. We have succeeded in avoiding this pecking-order of degrees and universities in this country, and it seems preferable to see this continued.

Finally, I am duty bound to sketch out, however briefly, a pattern that I believe would go some way to meeting the above conditions and answering the problems and paradoxes that have taken up the major part of this paper. It is because I want to see all these problems tackled together that I have dwelt so much longer on them than on the suggested solution below. I attach much less importance to the latter than to the recognition that it is the system as such that must be properly thought out.

My own proposal is to have a four-decker educational pattern rather than our present three-decker pattern of primary, secondary, and higher; to adopt the same age of transfer from primary to secondary schooling (namely eleven) in Scotland as in England; and to accept, in England as in Scotland, the level and breadth of SCE higher grade as the normal 'ceiling' for secondary education at the age of 16/17. After 16/17 there would be *two* further educational 'layers': first, a group of institutions for the 16/17-year-olds to the 19/20-year-olds which one might provisionally call tertiary colleges; and then, at the final stage, universities. These two groups of institutions would *not* be parallel, but rather 'end-on'.

In this pattern of education it is clearly the third stage, tertiary colleges, that needs definition and elucidation, because most of us are reasonably clear about what is meant by university education, whether undergraduate (honours) or postgraduate. As I see it, the tertiary college would be multi-purpose:

1 Covering for *two* years the kind of study in depth currently done in the Scottish sixth-form year and in English second- and third-year sixths, and so taking pupils to at least current A level standards. This would provide one method of university entry.
2 Covering in three to four years the work that is currently done to A level *and* covered by the first year (of a three-year honours course) of university studies. This would provide a second form of university entry, which would give a student access to the

university at the beginning of the second year of a three-year honours course.

3 Covering in anything from two to four years a whole range of courses in academic, technical, commercial, vocational, and liberal arts studies. These would give both general (tertiary) educational qualifications, as well as all kinds of professional and technical qualifications. In some cases the successful achievement of such qualifications could also lead to a third form of university entry, namely entry to the first or second year of a three-year degree course.

Under this scheme selection for university entrance would be 'phased', giving large numbers of aspiring students pre-university opportunities to discover their real academic bent and motivation, if any, without denying them avenues of tertiary and, later, university education. This would not only relieve the universities of numbers they are not at all likely to be able to cope with by 1980, but it would reduce some of the 'wastage' problems that currently beset them. It would also of course do much, by its 'end-on' pattern, to get rid of the more absurd aspects of the binary system.

This then is the debatable area and these are some of its problems. I believe they are insoluble without a radical restructuring of the whole pattern of education in Britain. Astronomically minded readers will recall that at the time of the Copernican revolution defenders of the Ptolemaic 'model' of the universe were forced into positing more and more 'epicycles' to make their theory tenable. British education today needs a Copernicus if it is to survive as a tenable system, for defenders of the system as it is cannot escape the fact that – to adapt Professor Flew's famous phrase – their faith in it faces death by a thousand epicyclic qualifications.

REFERENCES

BURGESS, TYRELL. *Times Educational Supplement* (Scotland), 23 October 1970 (see also leading article in that issue).

DREVER, JAMES. *Times Educational Supplement* (Scotland), 16 October 1970.

Role of the junior college

ALAN THOMPSON

This paper is based on the view that a new kind of institution is required in our educational system to act as a bridge between school and university. I appreciate that it is easier to suggest new institutions than to establish them, and that formidable difficulties lie in the path of the innovators. Furthermore, much more research is required into the problems of educational manpower and the measurement of educational productivity before we make major changes in the structure of higher education. This paper has the more limited aim of stimulating discussion on the need for a specific institution for certain educational objectives.

My interest in the idea of a junior college derived from a visit to the USA two years ago when I had the opportunity to observe the Californian system. It seemed to me to fill a need that was not being met under the British system, and I shall attempt to describe the system in more detail later in this paper. In doing so I am aware of the many differences between the British and American educational systems, and the undesirability of the one slavishly imitating the other. Nevertheless, international comparisons can serve to stimulate argument and reassessment. My interest was further stimulated by a period of service on the Scottish Committee of the Public Schools Commission. Having spent most of my adult life in university teaching (apart from five years under military discipline and another five under the more exacting discipline of the House of Commons) I soon discovered my ignorance of the current state of education at the pre-university level. One consequence of service on government committees of inquiry is that, in order to ask intelligent questions members have first to educate themselves.

In searching for some sort of pattern in post-16 education I realized that I was in a no man's land. The attitude of some universities (which I am glad to say has since improved) was one of indifference to how things were organized at the pre-university level so long as a reasonable supply of applicants ultimately presented themselves at the door of the university. The attitude of some teachers tended to be one of acute suspicion of any suggestion that disturbed the existing structure, particularly arrangements affecting the sixth form. It was partly to provoke discussion on this neglected area that I wrote a 'note of reservation' on the need for junior colleges as an appendix to the Public Schools Commission report (1970). In this I stated:

> In spite of the educational and social achievements of the all through (12–18) comprehensive school, I believe that more attention should be given to the long-term possibilities of a junior college system. The junior college, with its mixed intake of academic and non-academic students and covering a wide range of social classes, seems to me to meet all the requirements of a genuinely comprehensive educational system.

For those interested in the possibilities for Britain of a junior-college system, some description of the American system might be helpful. The example I have chosen is from California (although it must be borne in mind that California is considerably more advanced than most other states in this field). Apart from the internal organization of the junior college, certain features of its relationship with other educational levels deserve examination.

CALIFORNIAN EXPERIENCE IN JUNIOR-COLLEGE DEVELOPMENT

What is particularly interesting to the British observer is the attempt in California to frame a national plan for higher education in which universities, state colleges (four-year institutions), and junior colleges (two-year institutions) meet together to discuss and frame their plans for expansion, and maintain the closest liaison in such matters as academic objectives, student admission and transfer, and administrative control. This state-wide planning for higher education is done by the Coordinating Council for Higher Education, on which all types of institutions are represented.

California has had to face the problem that, in spite of its willingness to devote massive resources to higher education, it cannot meet its declared objective of 'higher education for everyone who can qualify' (and the qualifications are low by British standards) by concentrating solely on university expansion. Hence its decision to develop other kinds of institutions.

First, there are the state colleges (formerly mainly teachers' training colleges) which now pursue a wider range of advanced studies and grant degrees. They do not, however, award doctoral degrees and their research functions are strictly limited. It is felt that research funds would be dissipated if spread over too wide a range of institutions, and it is left to the universities to pursue higher research. This means that student costs are lower in state colleges, although every effort is made to preserve their status and efficiency, and they have a voice, through the Coordinating Council, in university affairs. Then, there are also provisions for transfer of students between the two types of institution and for the preparation of courses that facilitate such transfer.

It is the third level, however, that we are particularly interested in. It is in the junior college that California's attempt to provide the majority of its young citizens with higher education is most impressive.[1] It is doubtful whether any other area in the world has set itself such an ambitious and expensive target, and is achieving it with such speed. This attempt to secure higher education of good quality in terms of mass democracy may have valuable lessons for the British system. Its effects are to break down the class distinctions that often accompany educational differentiation, and to make the future technician and craftsman – who attend the same college along with those in the academic category – feel that they are as much part of a high-grade institution as the British university student does in this country.

The junior college is a two-year institution. It has a policy of almost unrestricted entry and is the means of providing post-high-school education for the maximum number of young persons. In fulfilling this function it meets the political demand of Californian citizens that all their children shall have access to higher education in some form. Some will later transfer from the junior college to degree-granting institutions like state colleges and universities, but the junior college also attempts to provide higher education for the vast number of young people who, while not wishing to take a degree, can nevertheless profit from training beyond the high school.

The junior college exists to serve three needs. The first is to give adequate opportunity for local students and to gear its programmes more closely to local industrial and economic conditions than universities tend to do. This is met by placing the colleges under a form of local control – a board of trustees directly elected by voters in the area in which the college is established. This gives citizens an interest and pride in the achievements of their college. The system has its dangers, particularly the interference by citizens in the internal affairs of the college. However, an able and persuasive college president (and the title and status accorded to the heads of colleges give them considerable local prestige) can do much to offset this hazard. Second, there is the need for facilities for students who prefer to do two years of their degree-course at the local junior college before transferring to a state college or university. This is much cheaper for the students (they have no residential costs and almost no tuition costs) and also for the state. It costs the state three times as much per student to provide a comparable two years at a university.

Third, there is the need to provide every high school district in the state with junior-college facilities.

The Californian master plan for higher education has devised a formula for all students graduating from high school. The upper $12\frac{1}{2}$ per cent of high-school graduates qualify for admission to the university; the upper $33\frac{1}{3}$ per cent qualify for admission to state colleges; all other high-school graduates can enter junior colleges, and those who do well enough can subsequently transfer to state colleges and universities.[2]

The overwhelming educational problem facing the junior college is whether its objective is too ambitious. Can it provide within a single institution the environment to sustain both the university-type programme and the terminal programme for students who will leave at the end of their two years? Is the range of capabilities represented in its student body too wide?

One college president to whom I spoke, Dr H. H. Semans, has no doubt that not only can the twin objectives be achieved in the same institution, but that students gain from cross-fertilization of ideas. He believes that junior colleges can be geared both to provide high-grade technical training for the skilled technicians and still to keep academic standards high enough for transfer students.

Dr Seman's institution, Foothill College, is designed for 4,500 day students. It has laboratories (it is a centre of training for the electronics industries), a planetarium and space-science centre.

An impressive aspect of the college's activities is its career-guidance programme. There are very few British institutions (although their number is increasing) which go to such lengths, and expense, to enable students to discover their aptitudes and choose their future training and careers.

Dr Semans refuses to admit that the junior college has an inferior status in California's educational plan. He sees it as one of three equal segments along with the state college and university. All three have specialized functions, but all have one common objective – to work together for the expansion of higher education in California. In his liaison meetings with state college and university representatives he refuses to talk about 'your' degree requirements. He deliberately talks about 'our' degree; as he says, junior colleges do nearly half the work anyway (of his 4,500 students 40 per cent proceed to degrees).

His policy is to integrate academic and vocational students in the same buildings, classrooms, laboratories, etc., so that no one can immediately differentiate the 'white collar' students from the 'blue collar trainees'. He insists on academic heads of departments taking a share of vocational instruction and all the career programmes are under 'academics'. He claims that his policy of integration has been highly successful, and other members of his college bear him out on this.

Certainly, the overall impression of Foothill is of a high quality collegiate environment such as a British university might well envy. It is largely, of course, the result of the generous economic resources devoted to the institution, but it also stems from the deliberate attempt to train future clerks, technicians, airline pilots, policemen, and health workers alongside future university graduates in a genuinely collegiate framework.

The Californian experiment is naturally geared to American needs and derives from American educational traditions. In certain limited respects, however, it may have something useful to teach Britain. Our higher educational system would benefit from closer cooperation and liaison among the different types of institutions. This could take the form of a coordinating council for higher education along the lines of the Californian model (with perhaps regional councils) on which universities and a variety of other institutions are represented.

The research function of the universities would, of course, be undisturbed and, like Californian practice, research would be a matter for university policy alone. As Professor Michael Swann, the recent Vice-Chancellor of the University of Edinburgh, has pointed out, there must be a place in our higher-education system for 'centres of excellence' in the field of research, and this is a task for universities. If Britain is to keep ahead in science and technological advance it must not allow the research functions of universities to be undermined or deprived of funds.

In the sphere of teaching, however, much could be gained by the exchange of ideas and by discussions on the allocation of educational functions. The Californian experience is that their council has fostered a new unity of purpose to those engaged at various levels in higher education.

The popularity of the junior college in the USA springs from several causes:

1 Its comprehensiveness and acceptance of virtually all applicants meet the demand for 'mass' higher education.
2 For 'transfer' students, it is an economical way of producing graduates (i.e. only half of their degree courses are taken at a full university or state college – both of which are more expensive institutions to run than the junior college).
3 Its administration is a mixture of state control and local government, which secures a measure of state subsidy while preserving local responsiveness to the needs of its area.

The objectives of the junior college are as follows:

1 To provide business, professional, and technical courses of a level somewhere between high school and state college (i.e., usually courses requiring a two-year training).
2 To provide courses for transfer students that are parallel with the requirements of universities and state colleges.
3 To provide general education courses for broadening educational and cultural experience.
4 To provide a second chance for late developers.
5 To provide counselling services to assist students in self-evaluation and attainment of their maximum potential (there is great emphasis on this).

6 To provide a diversified programme of community services for the recreational, cultural, and educational needs of the people of the district. (This programme is open to all citizens.)

Criticisms of the American system have been voiced on the grounds that the junior college gets everybody else's rejects. Other higher institutions, it is argued, have found a place to which they can refer all the people they do not want. The junior college, opening its arms to everyone, becomes the inheritor of all the problems the other institutions cannot or will not take on. Junior colleges, it is said, are faced with a student body containing too wide disparities in native capacity and performance. Finally, critics have argued that college staffs favour the academic side of their work and are hostile to the expansion of less prestigeful technical courses.

Most of these problems are probably financial in origin. Where state and local government are prepared to invest heavily in their junior-college system (as in California) their prestige increases and difficulties of staff recruitment are reduced. A genuine collegiate atmosphere prevails, and morale among staff and students is obviously higher.

The California junior-college system seems to possess two outstanding advantages. Quantitatively, it provides an avenue to higher education for the maximum number of young persons; qualitatively, it is experimenting with new types of interrelationships between vocational and other forms of education. Furthermore, within vocational education itself it is exploring the relationship between the strictly vocational content (both in the practical sense of acquiring specific skills and also the necessary theoretical content of such skills) and the more general educational side which is being increasingly included.

Nothing so ambitious and comprehensive as the Californian system has been suggested for Britain, but certain authorities are taking the first steps towards some form of junior colleges. Hampshire, is among the authorities that are introducing schemes, and it may be helpful to take its plan as a case study.

THE HAMPSHIRE SCHEME: THE COMPREHENSIVE COLLEGE

Although Hampshire's scheme is really a sixth-form college, it could at some future date be converted into a full junior college catering for the needs of a wider range of students than the academically able, although there are some difficulties involved in this change of role as we shall see.

The Hampshire story began when Circular 10/65 (requiring local authorities to prepare schemes for the organization of secondary education on a comprehensive pattern) was issued in July 1965. It was not until October 1967, however, that the Education Committee finally made a recommendation to the County Council for the introduction of a general policy of comprehensive secondary education. The preceding two years had been spent considering, with representatives of the authority's teachers, the educational implications of reorganization.

The conclusions reached after this consideration were that the Education Committee's policies of building large bilateral schools, encouraging all secondary schools to offer a wide range of academic and non-academic courses to their pupils up to the age of sixteen, and welcoming the rapid growth of, and more flexible entry to, the sixth forms of grammar schools could be most soundly developed through the alternative comprehensive patterns set out below:

1 straight-through comprehensive schools catering for all pupils from 11, later 12, to 18 or
2 comprehensive schools catering for all pupils from 11, later 12, to 16, linked with comprehensive colleges for students over 16.

The Education Committee recommended that no date should be set for the preparation or implementation of schemes nor for the change in the age of transfer, but that schemes should be prepared and changes introduced on an area basis in the light of what seemed best educationally for each area. These recommendations were approved by the County Council on 1 January 1968. Then, on 30 June 1970, came the issue by Mrs Thatcher of the famous Circular 10/70. It should be noted, however, that despite its proclaimed policies and circulars, the former government had made no attempt to exert direct pressure on Hampshire to prepare a complete scheme for the whole county nor to hasten the implementation of the schemes prepared. The Schools Sub-Committee at its meeting on 7 July welcomed, however, the formal restoration in Circular10/70 of local authorities' freedom to decide the pattern of secondary education for their areas in the light of educational and local needs. The Sub-Committee felt too that as these factors had always guided it, it should recommend that present proposals for reorganization should be endorsed and that proposals for the few remaining parts of the county should be framed in the same manner and on the same educational basis as had been observed in preparing existing schemes.

In a recent report the Director of Education for Hampshire (Mr Robert Marsh) described how the existing schemes are working.

Comprehensive schools cover at least a five-year course, and so it is too early to report on progress being made in those areas where reorganization has already taken place except to say that the transfer of pupils to secondary schools has taken place much more smoothly in these areas than in those where selection is still practised.

The two comprehensive colleges at Totton and Brockenhurst, on the other hand, offer courses for one, two, and three years. Although they began their development only in September 1969 it is possible to give some idea of the progress which they are already making.

Post fifth year intakes in September:	*1968*	*1969*	*1970*	*1971* (*anticipated*)
Totton	90	152	224	219
Brockenhurst	291	347	406	331
	(including 69 who were at Christchurch Grammar School)			

The principals of both colleges report a dramatic increase in the interest shown by sixteen-year-olds from other schools to enter the colleges. This interest is reflected, for example, in the intake to Totton College from its own and other schools over the last three years.

	Admitted from	
	own school	*elsewhere*
1968	71	19
1969	76	76
1970	97	127
1971 (anticipated)	97	122

Brockenhurst Grammar School had already established a tradition of fairly large-scale admission at sixteen plus, but even so the growth in 1970 was remarkable:

Total admissions	*406*

From Brockenhurst	137
From elsewhere	269

At both colleges the broad range of GCE advanced level courses previously offered by the grammar schools has been maintained and is now being offered both more widely and more flexibly to many more students. Alongside these courses have been developed associated courses at the ordinary level of GCE to broaden the base of students' education. Courses in business studies and preparatory studies for nurses and medical auxiliaries are also being linked with ordinary and advanced level studies where this is appropriate for the students. Links with neighbouring technical colleges are being developed in accordance with the Education Committee's declared policy.

With regard to future plans Mr Marsh states:

> The Education Committee's recommendation for the establishment of an all-purpose college in Andover takes a stage further the policy of close cooperation between comprehensive and technical colleges. It advocates, in order to provide the widest possible educational opportunities and the best use of resources available, the development in a new purpose-built college of appropriate courses for all post-16-year-old students on both a fulltime and parttime basis.

The Hampshire plan, with its comprehensive schools for the 11 to 16 age-range and its comprehensive colleges for pupils over 16 is significant for two reasons. Educationally, it introduces a new post-16 structure. Politically, it is an interesting compromise. Selection at 11 has been abolished, but at the same time the academic content of the grammar school is retained at the point where it is most needed. The grammar schools do not disappear, their curriculum is enlarged and the opportunity given to all children who wish to attend to do so. Socialist councillors have applauded the abolition of selection. Conservatives have claimed that the best traditions of the grammar school have been preserved. Reorganization took place step by step and considerable care was taken to consult both parent and teacher.

As a political exercise, the Hampshire scheme is a model to other authorities in Britain.

THE JUNIOR COLLEGE IN SCOTLAND

The question arises of how applicable is the Hampshire scheme to Scotland?

Some of its advantages apply equally to the Scottish situation, e.g., the economical use of high-cost equipment in such subjects as physics, chemistry, engineering, etc., and of scarce specialist teachers. It also gives us the opportunity to treat senior pupils as young adults rather than as children. This argument seems to me as compelling as the economic and educational reasons. Educational structure should respond to the changing character and attitudes of the younger generation of the 1970s. The sixth-form pupils of the future will be very different from those of the 1950s. They will have inherited many of the attitudes to life of the present generation of university students, and just as universities are having to respond to these new conditions, so will other echelons of higher education have to meet the challenge very soon. Aspirations to 'student power' will soon be succeeded by 'sixth-form power'. This fact is understood by many headmasters in both the maintained and grant-aided sectors. Nevertheless, the atmosphere of a junior college would meet their needs more adequately. This theme was developed in my 'note of reservation' to the Public Schools Commission (1970):

> The coming generation of over-16s will have one experience in common with the present university generation: it will have grown up in comparative affluence, free from the anxieties of unemployment and poverty which older generations had to face. While this may have made young people self-indulgent, it has freed them from the preoccupation of an older generation with the acquisition of material things and the sometimes dehumanising endeavours to acquire wealth and status. Inevitably, it has made them less responsive to discipline. The affluence of recent years has given them confidence that they can always make a living. Although the ties of family, tradition and financial responsibility are weak, their attitude to life is often marked by open-mindedness and generosity.
>
> This is the generation that will offer educationalists perhaps their greatest challenge, and I am convinced that a system of

education based on the junior college (although such a change can be introduced only gradually) offers the best solution.

Another advantage lies in the contribution that a junior-college system could make towards university education. This is, however, a new and complex area of discussion and will be dealt with separately below.

As a long-term proposal, the junior-college system could save Scotland the expense of a national system of all-through comprehensive schools. A system of, say, twelve–sixteen comprehensive schools (there is room for argument over the exact age-ranges) and junior colleges could utilize smaller schools, instead of very large comprehensives, and would fit more easily into present buildings.

Scotland would admittedly face similar problems to those of Hampshire in extending the sixth-form nucleus to include vocational training of a technical and specialist nature and incorporating education and training for mature students. Colleges of further education could argue that their facilities could take care of these needs without the necessity of a new type of institution (although it could be argued that these colleges might themselves become the nucleus of junior-college development). A serious problem also arises in the more sparsely populated areas of Scotland, where there would not be enough staff to deal with the range of vocational needs. If the colleges concentrated on 'liberal' education the problem would not be so acute; indeed, it might help to stem the criticism made in many rural areas that children have to go away to school at too early an age (i.e. eleven to twelve). If there was a middle school from about ten-plus to fourteen-plus it might be possible for smaller communities to support a middle school, since they would not require the services of such highly qualified teachers.

Nevertheless, in both rural and urban areas I would be reluctant to see the abandonment of the idea of a junior college as an institution that combined academic and vocational courses, on both a full-time and parttime basis.[3] At present, it can be argued, the worst form of selection occurs at 16. Academic students stay on at school, and students of a vocational bent proceed to technical colleges. Why not, therefore, put all students over 16 into one separate institution? The outstanding feature of the Californian-type college, as we saw above, was the sense of community created for students of all types and from all social classes, and the genuinely collegiate atmosphere that prevailed. To British eyes, this was a most impressive and exciting achievement.

The age of transfer creates some difficulties for Scotland (unless, as Roger Young suggests, we move towards a unified British educational system). If the age of transfer is 16, this would mean that most of the able pupils would have already sat their Scottish Certificate of Education ordinary grade examinations in the feeder school. Therefore, the teachers in the junior colleges would have only one year in which to get to know them and prepare them for the SCE higher grades. A better age of transfer in Scotland might be the end of the third year (i.e., at the age of fifteen or fifteen-plus). This would have the advantage of enabling pupils to study for two years before they embarked on their 'highers' and it would also ensure that every boy and girl had experience of the new college situation before he or she reached school-leaving age. The reason for stressing this point is that, at present, many pupils leave at the end of the third year because of the restrictions of traditional discipline in the ordinary school.

Other difficulties involved in introducing a junior-college system (some common to both England and Scotland) must obviously be faced. A few of these are stated below, and the list is by no means exhaustive:

1 What will be the optimal size? It has been argued that a school of fewer than 1,000 pupils is uneconomic. (It is true that the term 'uneconomic' begs a number of questions – what is the unit of output of an educational system? is it a 'pupil' or is it 'a unit of good education'? – nevertheless, government policy accepts some rough and ready concept of 'optimum' so far as size is concerned.)
    Numbers are clearly important: they determine the range of courses that can be offered, and this variety is crucial to the concept of the junior college.
2 What will be the effects on all-through schools? It could be argued that a junior-college system would sever the mature head from the body so far as these schools are concerned. Pupils look to senior pupils for leadership. On the other hand it might be argued that 'leadership' is restricted under the present system strictly to 'academic' pupils. American experience shows that leadership can be provided by a wide range of students, both academic and vocational.

3 It might make staff recruitment to all-through schools more difficult.
4 Arising from 3 above it would probably be opposed by teacher organizations. They might feel that it introduced yet another distinction of status into the teaching profession. Difficulties would also arise over the salary structure if higher remuneration were proposed for junior-college staffs. If university transfer students were also taught (as suggested below) would not these teachers expect university rates? Certainly, the trend in American junior colleges has been to move their teaching staffs (whether academic or vocational) towards university status, both in pay and conditions. University titles ('president', 'dean', 'faculty', etc.) are used in Californian junior colleges.
5 Difficulties will arise in accommodating a junior-college system to the present Scottish examination structure.[4]

RELATIONSHIP WITH THE UNIVERSITY

A junior-college system could help in reducing the pressure on the universities. In many subjects, it should be possible for students to complete at least one year of their undergraduate course at a junior college. This would cut the cost of undergraduate training, both through the lower overheads of non-research-type institutions and the fact that students would probably live at home in their first year. There are problems about recognition by the university of courses provided by junior colleges but these difficulties can be exaggerated. When adequate liaison exists, as it does in the California system, excellent relations exist between the two levels, and the universities profit from their involvement in discussing the problems (educational, social, and economic) of the pre-university educational structure. This liaison has led to considerable rationalization of higher education, to a reduction in costs, to the abolition of the haphazard system that existed previously in some areas, and to a more sensible allocation of functions to different types of institution. The junior college (which a few decades ago was regarded with suspicion) is now the main recognized route to university education. Much more research is required on all these topics. Yet it is surely worth the cost. A junior college–university alliance in higher education averts the major criticisms levelled at the present binary system by Roger Young.

CONCLUSION

The educational and social advantages (as well as the difficulties) of the junior-college system have been examined at length. Only two further points remain to be made. First, innovation and experiment in educational systems should not be condemned out of hand. The Hampshire experiment shows the advantages of diversity and flexibility in educational arrangements, and may suggest new forms of reorganization to local authorities which have previously believed that no further thought or discussion was required on the subject of educational objectives.

Second, the junior-college system may provide an escape from the present political *impasse*. Again, the Hampshire experiment shows the wisdom of allowing an authority some flexibility in its educational policy. Its plans have survived a change of government and continue to enjoy the support of all the political parties. By using the experience and resources of its former grammar schools in an intelligent and imaginative way its policy enjoys the support of the conservatives: by pursuing a non-selective junior-college policy it satisfies labour that it is a genuinely comprehensive scheme. It is true that, in the comprehensive sense, it would be improved by the inclusion of vocational students, but the present 'unsystematic jumble' of 16 to 21 education (to quote Mr Young) makes this a long-term objective. The junior college (or community, or comprehensive college – the name is not important) could be a bridge therefore not merely between different levels of education but between opposing educational philosophies. If our educational system is to be subjected to the violent stress and upheaval of major change at regular five-year intervals, this latter objective could be the most crucial. It is an intolerable situation for teachers, parents, and pupils that the entire educational system should be threatened with disruption every time the government of the country changes hands. Something must be done to stop the present hardening of party political attitudes to educational reform. The junior-college proposals may be a modest step towards starting a sensible dialogue between opposing viewpoints.

NOTES

[1] The name 'junior college' has since been replaced in California by 'community college'.

[2] The Legislature is considering a recommendation of the Coordinating Council for Higher Education that applicants from junior colleges who have completed the necessary work shall have first priority for admission to the state colleges and the state university. This means in effect that the junior college would be the main recognized route for admission to higher levels of education in California, and will further enhance its status and effectiveness.

[3] See Public Schools Commission, *Report*, p. 151.

[4] See Public Schools Commission, *Report*, p. 152.

REFERENCE

PUBLIC SCHOOLS COMMISSION. 1970. *Report*. Vol. III (Scotland). Appendix 14. London: HMSO.

Colleges of education in the seventies

SIR HENRY WOOD

I should like to consider the education of teachers generally, not just in colleges of education, and I shall deal with this from a United Kingdom standpoint, and not concentrate on the Scottish situation only.

Before the end of this century, we shall have ten million boys and girls in our school system and half a million teachers. It will be a colossal operation and it will always be controversial. There is no prospect of an easing off in the attention that schooling will demand from the community – from politicians, from bureaucrats, from universities, from colleges of all kinds, from the teachers themselves, from parents, from employers, from all kinds of voluntary organizations that care about the quality of personal and corporate life. The key to good schooling lies in a continuous supply of good teachers which is partly an administrative problem, partly a problem in the field of liberal higher education, with both issues continually changing their form in a technological society. To find answers demands agreement about the scale of the operation and acceptance by the parties concerned of their proper functions within it.

The scale of the operation is large (there will be at any given time over 120,000 students training to be teachers) and such an important public enterprise will always engage a corresponding measure of government attention, both political and bureaucratic.

The parties concerned in the operation are the universities, the colleges of education, and a whole range of central institutions, polytechnics and monotechnics. One of the fundamental problems to be resolved in the 1970s must be the relationship of these partners in the enterprise and whether or not the universities can or should accept the major responsibility in this field.

The other fundamental question is the quality of the education of teachers which cannot be dissociated from the extent to which curriculum development, as we now know it in primary and secondary education, will be extended to tertiary education as a whole and so lead to an examination of what to teach modern students and how to do it.

I shall attempt to illustrate these two problems by a consideration of colleges of education as they have developed up to 1970 and of the current proposals for change and reform, but first of all it is necessary to remind ourselves of the essential differences between the English and Scottish systems (see Wood 1964).

In 1961 the professional training of teachers in Scotland was conducted in seven colleges of education – a comprehensive day-college in each of the four university cities, residential colleges for Catholic women in Glasgow and Edinburgh, and a College of Physical Education for Women in Aberdeen. The student population was 6,200 of whom 82 per cent were women and 17 per cent graduates. There was *one* system of training and the universities were not responsible for the training of teachers. The university Departments of Education were centres of advanced study for the degree of Bachelor of Education (now Master of Education) which had been established in 1920 and had no counterpart in England. The colleges had achieved a considerable degree of academic autonomy; they had direct financial links with the Scottish Education Department and were governed by Boards on which teachers were strongly represented. By English standards the four colleges in the cities were very large and they had a statutory responsibility for the in-service training of teachers. In England there were *two* systems of training – the university system (university departments for postgraduate training) and the training-college system linked for academic purposes with the university institutes of education created as a result of the McNair report. There were 24 UDEs, 120 general training colleges, eighteen homecraft colleges, seven physical education colleges, fifteen art-training centres, and four technical teacher-training colleges – in all 188 institutions dealing with 40,000 students of whom 65 per cent were women and 8·5 per cent graduates. The colleges were conducted by local education authorities or voluntary bodies, and were still inspected by the

Ministry of Education. The general colleges trained teachers in two-year courses for work in secondary schools whereas in Scotland only university graduates were trained for this work.

Robbins recommended that training in England should be conducted by schools of education based on universities and that in both countries colleges should institute BEd degrees in association with universities, and finance should be provided for the colleges through a grants committee similar to the University Grants Committee. Since Robbins the universities have developed BEd degree courses despite preoccupation with their own expansion, but only Birmingham and Bristol have accepted the more extensive commitment of schools of education. By government decree the binary system of higher education was confirmed and no committees of the UGC type have been established.

Both systems have expanded greatly since 1963, and in 1968 the student enrolment in colleges was 118,500: in England 106,500, in Scotland 12,000.

The important development in Scotland since 1963 has been the opening of three new colleges for the training of primary teachers. The new colleges, Craigie (Ayr) and Callendar Park (Falkirk), opened in 1964, and Hamilton opened in 1966; all three, with young and enthusiastic staffs able to devote all their energies to one task, primary education, were able to take advantage of the official blessing given in *Primary Education in Scotland* (1965) to a more progressive approach to primary teaching. New courses were developed with emphasis on both the extension of the education of the student and a fresh approach to preparing teachers for a more child-centred discovery type of teaching. All the colleges gained a ready response from the primary schools in their areas and new forms of staff/student/teacher cooperation have developed in connection with both in-service training and the opportunities that colleges could provide for musical, dramatic, and other cultural activities in county areas. Three of the older colleges, Aberdeen, Notre Dame, and Dunfermline College of Physical Education, have moved into new buildings and extension of the other colleges is in progress.

In England the three-year courses have become firmly established and the colleges have therefore become much larger than formerly. Some day-colleges have been established and a smaller proportion of all the colleges are now single-sex establishments.

In Scotland, for the first time since 1928, apart from the Emergency Training Scheme after the war, men have been admitted to the three-year courses but not, as in England, to courses leading to secondary teaching.

The pattern of BEd courses has followed different lines. In England the transition to a three-subject BEd (with 'education' subsuming as one subject what the Scots would describe as education, psychology, and methods) was relatively easy because of the strong tradition of main courses in the colleges. In Scotland, the degrees instituted at Aberdeen, Edinburgh, and Glasgow have tended to follow the traditional Scottish ordinary MA pattern, but the Dundee scheme allows progress from the diploma course to the degree course for students of proved ability. There has been some disappointment that all the colleges have not been permitted to begin BEd courses and also that subjects like physical education have not found favour with the universities as readily as in England.

In England the institution of compulsory training for graduates is promised for 1973, and many colleges of education have begun to offer courses for graduates. This process seems likely to expand since the university departments of education do not appear to welcome massive expansion of their present intake.

The colleges of education in the south have all been taking action to implement the recommendations of the Weaver report on the government of colleges and the participation of staff in boards of studies as well as in decisions on educational policy. Much of this was already in existence in Scotland as a result of the 1958 regulations. In both countries considerable attention has been given to student participation in college government and academic activities. In this sphere progress in the south has possibly been more rapid.

Further education in Scotland has expanded rapidly during this decade and the training of teachers for the further education colleges has accordingly developed very substantially in the School of Further Education at Jordanhill.

The diversification of the commitments of colleges in Scotland has occurred mainly at Moray House and Jordanhill where courses for social workers and for youth and community workers have been established. Jordanhill has also undertaken the training of speech therapists. Some colleges in England have introduced youth work as part of their normal activities.

The establishment of a concurrent degree and teacher-training course at the University of Stirling, on the lines of the courses at Keele, has been a departure from normal Scottish practice. It is too early to say whether this course will make a significant contribution to the supply of teachers for Scottish schools.

In Scotland the establishment of the General Teaching Council in 1965, with its duty to act as the main adviser to the Secretary of State on standards of entry to the teaching profession and on courses of instruction leading to the award of a teaching qualification, and its right to visit colleges, has meant that the teaching profession, always strongly represented on boards of governors, has increased its influence on teacher training.

While no firm decisions or definite steps have yet been taken to change the nature and functions of colleges of education in the 1970s, there has been much activity in the last two years and this will eventually lead to change. Evidence has been taken by a Select Committee of the House of Commons (1970a, 1970b); the National Union of Teachers has produced two reports (1969, 1970); the Association of Teachers in Colleges and Departments of Education has produced documents indicating the views of those most intimately concerned in this question (1970); various groups associated with the Royal Society have reported about the training of science teachers (1969, 1970); and a Nuffield investigation has been established. On the government side the Scottish Education Department has issued a memorandum (1970) on the training of graduates for secondary schools, and the present Minister for Education and Science has asked the area training authorities for views and is appointing a small committee to be chaired by Lord James to report on teacher training.

In considering some of the views now current it is perhaps worth remembering the tendency of both England and Scotland to see virtues in a system or practice that the other country would like to discard.

The very definite and direct views of the Association of Teachers in Colleges and Departments of Education are as follows:

1 As soon as practicable and certainly not later than 1980, candidates entering the colleges direct from school should have at least the minimum qualification required for university entrance.

2 The colleges should take at least a proportionate share in the expansion of the system of higher education.
3 Colleges should be grouped into federated units and each group affiliated in special relationship to a university.
4 As many universities as possible should participate in these special relationship arrangements.
5 Where they have the resources to do so the colleges should offer three-year courses leading to first degrees in the Faculties of Arts, Science, and Social Science, and a variety of professional postgraduate courses, as well as concurrent BEd and Certificate courses. The following figure shows the proposed structure of college courses.

FIGURE 1   Proposed structure of college courses

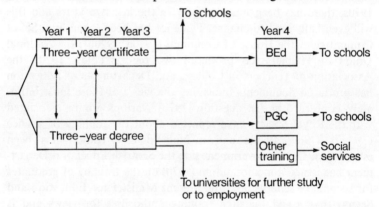

NOTE: The above scheme should be regarded as an example of the kind of flexibility that could be developed within college courses over the next decade. Variations on the general pattern would be possible in different colleges. Some might arrange to have the first two years of all courses in common and thus delay the 'branching' until the end of the second year. Others might more easily organize some elements common to both routes and thus facilitate exchange and transfer. Other colleges might adopt the principle that a satisfactory course is an approved combination of shorter courses and provide a wide range of these courses in years one and two from which students would choose combinations appropriate to their developing interests and/or vocational goals. Students would thus have the opportunity to exercise a measure of control over the total course they build for themselves out of the range of shorter courses available. Much would depend on the size of the providing institution since this would determine the number of staff and thus the range of courses that would be offered.

6 The colleges within each group should rationalize the use of their resources under the guidance of the university.

7 The colleges within each group should, with the guidance of the university, develop in ways that best suit their particular circumstances and the general policy for the development of higher education in the area.

8 Students should be given the opportunity to delay their commitment to teaching if they so wish.

9 Ultimately recruitment to the teaching profession should be limited to graduates.

10 All institutions of higher education should be financed on the same principles. As a step towards this the colleges urge the early establishment of a centralized Colleges Grants Committee to finance the work of the colleges.

The colleges clearly wish to maintain a strong university link (but not to become part of universities) and to break the financial and administrative link with local education authorities. They also wish to become liberal arts colleges but they have definite views on the nature of the degrees. ATCDE (1970) envisages the colleges making a distinctive contribution to the range of undergraduate courses rather than offering a replica of traditional honours courses.

The colleges have considerable experience of inter-disciplinary and grouped courses and have traditionally placed great emphasis on the quality of their teaching, though not to the exclusion of further study and research. They could well meet a real need by developing broadly based courses in the sciences, the humanities, the creative arts and social and behavioural studies, which would permit a considerable element of inter-disciplinary study. Such courses, terminating with a degree award, would provide a satisfactory higher education for those who could work at the level of a first degree. These courses would also be eminently suitable for the many students who would see their degrees as preparation for professional postgraduate courses of various kinds including teaching.

The National Union of Teachers is also anxious to preserve the university connection with teacher training though with a difference, or a number of differences. It presses for the Robbins university school of education with an academic board responsible to the university for both degree and certificate work and then proposes that the schools of education should each have an advisory council composed of representatives of the local education authorities in the area, the teachers' associations, the individual colleges associated with the school, the academic boards of the colleges, the student bodies of the colleges, and a representative of the Secretary of State as an assessor.

The great difference between the ATCDE and the NUT is that the latter accepts Pedley-ism applied to higher education (1969):

. . . in the long term, on educational as well as administrative grounds, higher education should be organised on the basis of the 'comprehensive university', organised and administered on a regional basis and coordinated nationally. Each region (comprising an area as large or larger than the unitary authority area suggested in the Redcliffe–Maud Report on Local Government) would be the geographical and educational basis for each comprehensive university. The present separation of higher education into three sectors, universities, colleges of education and colleges for further education, is socially and educationally divisive, as well as being exceptionally wasteful and uneconomic in the use of staff, buildings, laboratories and libraries, sporting and social facilities. It is unlikely that future generations will accept that the continuance of the present arrangements will meet their needs and aspirations. The following statement by Professor Pedley explains briefly the concept of the comprehensive university, 'a comprehensive system provides a great variety of studies and activities to meet the multitude of individual needs, and does so within a basic unity. It is this unity which facilitates flexible arrangements, ease of movement between courses, co-operative policy-making and planning and full rationalisation of resources; and thereby makes possible the reduction and eventual elimination of unjust and unjustifiable social and educational barriers'.

The NUT urges closer cooperation between colleges of education and polytechnics or the incorporation of polytechnics into area training organizations, and clearly looks forward to the closing and total elimination of many small colleges of education. While the NUT agrees with the idea of expanding the provision for BEd, looking forward to 50 per cent of the college population by 1975 and 100 per cent by the 1980s taking the degree, it is critical of the existing arrangements whereby fourteen universities expect normal matriculation, four insist on a special examination, and only four accept the Teachers' Certificate as an entry qualification. There is also a demand for classified honours degrees in order to satisfy the teachers' case for salary awards, promotion, and access to higher degrees. The need for a four-year college of education course as well as for end-on postgraduate training is accepted, but the Union appears to see little future for the university departments of education:

> Under the system proposed there would appear to be little point in the university departments of education continuing to under-take the professional training of the majority of newly qualified graduates. This task could be carried out by the colleges of the Schools of Education which would be more suitably staffed and equipped to provide the type of training that the young graduate needs. University departments of education have a tendency to look upon teacher education as a discipline rather than as a means of providing professional expertise. There is no reason why university faculties of education should not continue to have a role in special areas of education and educational research.

While the ATCDE policies could, in the main, be achieved by developing existing patterns and arrangements, it is clear that attempts to implement the NUT's views would lead to tremendous upheaval and power struggles on finance and control, on the expansion of some large colleges of education and the closure of others, on the relationships between universities of the existing pattern and publicly controlled comprehensive universities which, whatever they might become, would not be universities in the English tradition.

Mrs Thatcher has asked the area training organizations to under-take a major review of the content and structure of courses. She intends that teachers, local authorities, and students should be associated with the review. In her letter to teachers' unions and associations in connection with training, on the question of the form of the short intensive inquiry by a committee that Lord James is to conduct, the Minister expresses the hope that ways will be found of breaking down the isolation of colleges of education 'so that a growing proportion of intending teachers are trained side by side with students, who are either vocationally uncommitted or committed to other careers. This will inevitably involve the committee in a wider consideration of what, in relation to the training of teachers, should be the roles of colleges of education, polytechnics and other further education colleges and universities.' There is no sign of a general review of the whole higher education system or of the abandonment of the LEA and voluntary system of conducting colleges of education.

Where does Scotland stand in relation to all these conflicting views and aspirations?

In the first place there have been no reports and pressures of the kind generated by the ATDCE and the NUT. Colleges of education, teachers, students, and education authorities submitted their views to the Select Committee and presumably these will be considered by the General Teaching Council when it presents its views to the Secretary of State for Scotland. Certainly there is no policy in Scotland for colleges of education to contribute, other than through the professional training element of expanding higher education, to the needs of higher education in the 1970s. It is tacitly assumed that liberal arts colleges are unnecessary and that existing universities can cope with expansion especially because of the potential for growth of the newer universities, Strathclyde, Heriot-Watt, Dundee, and Stirling. Thus, the course structures for colleges adumbrated by the ATDCE, though certainly possible in Scotland, have not been considered.

There has been no pressure from universities to establish schools of education similar to that in Bristol, though one or two people would like to see university departments of education established, and some subject departments in universities would like to become involved in chemical education or mathematical education with a view to increasing the supply of specialist teachers for the upper secondary schools. Certainly greater university control of teacher education would mean less teacher control and perhaps this is why the NUT espouses the comprehensive university and asks for advisory councils similar to the boards of governors of Scottish colleges.

In Scotland a graduate profession has always been an aim (almost achieved in 1931), but the teaching profession has always seen this as occurring through traditional MA and BSc university courses or central institution courses (art, music, etc.) and not through colleges of education. Indeed, the BEd has gained grudging acceptance from the Scottish teachers and the only college (Dundee) that has attempted to follow the Robbins, English, pattern by basing the degree on the three-year course in a college of education is regarded with a great deal of suspicion by the teachers and the other BEd students. Naturally one of the reasons for this situation is the continued preponderance of ordinary degrees in the Scottish universities. There are pressures from staff and students in colleges of education for easier transfer from diploma to BEd courses and also for the institution of a common first-year degree course after which students would decide to opt for teaching or social work or youth work. Such things are not easy to achieve under the existing BEd structures, and common first-year courses are not easy to devise for people with disparate qualifications and backgrounds. At present only four of the ten Scottish colleges offer BEd courses, and the six other colleges have recently put a strong case to the General Teaching Council for support in their demand to be permitted to initiate degree courses.

The Scottish colleges of education have always been independent of local education authorities but there are those who would see in the creation of the new super education authorities an opportunity for taking over control of colleges of education and of central institutions.

The Scottish colleges of education have been financed from central authority funds for a long time, and it would not appear to be difficult to establish a grants committee to overlook the whole operation and to assist the Scottish Education Department in its negotiations with the Treasury.

It is interesting to speculate on what might have happened in the past and on what still might happen in the future. I have always felt that Robbins was wrong about the BEd and that he should have recommended the American system of college degrees, which would have enabled specialist institutions to give a degree for their own normal activity and avoid aspirations about university status. I have never thought, for instance, that Jordanhill should be a university but I do think that it could quite well give Bachelors degrees. I have always been attracted too by the concept of the University of the State of New York which has no campus but consists of an association of seventy colleges of various kinds which give degree courses in engineering, agriculture, art, education, and so on under the general direction of a Board of Regents of the University. One could imagine Jordanhill, Notre Dame, and all the central institutions in Glasgow operating as a University of the City of Glasgow. Alternatively, if there can be a Bath University of Technology, why couldn't there be a Scottish University of Education or, in the west, a Stow University of Education comprising Jordanhill, Notre Dame, Craigie, and Hamilton?

These idle speculations are not likely to be taken seriously. I am not myself averse to university schools of education in Scotland and university control of teacher education provided that what is being considered is the whole undertaking and not certain subject specializations or superior types of students. The size of Scottish colleges and the continued existence of denominational colleges does not make the implementation of suggestions of this kind easy for universities or for colleges.

May I say a word finally about the quality of teacher education and begin by asserting simply that after thirty-four years' experience in colleges and universities in England and Scotland I am satisfied that there has been a great improvement in the quality of training in my professional lifetime.

The educational arguments for change are concerned with curriculum development (curriculum innovation), and the decline in the acceptability of subjects or what used to be described as academic disciplines; with the growth of comprehensivization (progressive participatory education which will have repercussions on higher education and the universities as well as on primary and secondary schools), a move from what the psychologist Eric Fromm would term paternalistic education to maternalistic education; and the educational technology movement, computer-assisted learning, and so on, which is something very different from using machines of all kinds as aids to traditional teaching. I do not know of any college that is not wrestling with these problems despite difficulties of staffing, space, and finance. The difficulty is to prepare the primary teacher to succeed in a first post that might be in a rigidly traditional school, or in a school that is traditional but thinks it is progressive, or in a really progressive school. In secondary training the difficulty is to prepare academics and specialists to teach new subjects in new ways to future academics, and at the same time to prepare them to share in the 'education of the whole people' which is the task of the new secondary school.

Greater participation by teachers in the training of graduates formed part of the proposals in the Scottish Education Department's memorandum on the *Training of Graduates for Secondary Schools* which one anticipates will be given further consideration by the General Teaching Council. I am all in favour of the greater participation of teachers in training but I am not certain how effective this can be until staffing is less precarious.

I am not impressed either by the NUT argument about the 'communion of students' or by Mrs Thatcher's desire to mix intending teachers with people doing other things. I have found over the years that students who have been at the same university for three or four years have not achieved 'communion' – the chemists do not know the mathematicians and the classics do not know the modern linguists. What the university has to offer is not communion (this is perhaps part of a nineteenth-century Oxbridge myth that what matters is who you meet and not what you learn) but facilities for independent student life away from the teaching and learning process and a greater measure of detachment about the progress, attitudes, and welfare of students than is possible in a purely professional institution.

I suspect that students are really less worried about communion than anxious to postpone professional commitment and their arguments may be met by providing degree courses, provided that this does not mean impairing the quality of good certificate or diploma courses, nor involve either a diminution of the aesthetic and practical aspects of education which many teachers need or the production of graduates who know nothing but politics, sociology, and psychology.

Generally speaking colleges of education have never had much say about their role in the sphere of higher education – this has been determined by regulations about teacher training and by the appropriate ministries – and, apart from excursions into the social-work field, the colleges have not been allowed or encouraged to depart from their traditional role. This traditional role has, I think, been fulfilled with distinction during the last decade. The teacher-training sector, more than any other sector of higher education, has had to meet the phenomenal explosion in educational provision that was initiated by the postwar Education Acts. The increase in the number of students in colleges of education has been incomparably greater than the increases in the other sectors of higher education. To this must be added the development of the BEd degree, the contribution to curriculum innovation in primary and secondary schools, and, especially in Scotland, the very considerable provision of in-service courses for teachers. These are quite remarkable achievements, quantitatively and qualitatively, in a decade when supply considerations were paramount and financial resources, at times, severely restricted.

The colleges, which must be the most cost-effective sector of higher education, could play an equally effective role in higher education in the 1970s if the discussions and investigations now in progress produce appropriate development plans.

REFERENCES

ASSOCIATION OF TEACHERS IN COLLEGES AND DEPARTMENTS OF EDUCATION. 1970. *Higher Education and Preparation for Teaching.* London: ATCDE.

NATIONAL UNION OF TEACHERS. 1969. *The Future of Teacher Education* (National Young Teacher Advisory Committee). London: NUT.

——1970. *Teacher Education – The Way Ahead.* London: NUT.

NUFFIELD FOUNDATION. *Science Teacher Education.*

ROYAL SOCIETY. 1970. *Teachers for Science and Mathematics Graduates.* London: Royal Society.

ROYAL SOCIETY AND INSTITUTE OF PHYSICS. 1969. *Teacher Training for Physics Graduates.* London: Royal Society.

SCOTTISH EDUCATION DEPARTMENT. 1965. *Primary Education in Scotland.* Edinburgh: SED.

——1970. *The Training of Graduates for Secondary Teaching.* Edinburgh: SED.

SELECT COMMITTEE ON EDUCATION AND SCIENCE. 1970a. *Teacher Training.* London: HMSO.

—— 1970b. (Scottish sub-committee) *Teacher Training.* London: HMSO.

WOOD, H. P. 1964. Teacher Training in England and Scotland. *Advancement of Science*, 1964.

The other side of the binary system

JOHN LOWE

Until 1960 or thereabouts higher education was almost exclusively identified with the universities, which did not pretend to be other than elitist institutions. Apart from the universities' sphere of interest the tertiary field of education appeared shapeless and lacked status. Officially it was known as further education, that is, formal education designed for those who had passed beyond the compulsory school-leaving age and who were not attending universities,[1] and it referred to a wide range of academic levels and to the provisions of a multitude of institutions bearing a confusing variety of names. It was chiefly administered by local education authorities under the terms of Section 41 of the 1944 Education Act, which defined its province as follows:

(a) full-time and part-time education for persons over compulsory school age; and
(b) leisure-time occupation, in such organized cultural training and recreative activities as are suited to their requirements, for any persons over compulsory school age who are able and willing to profit . . .

The Scottish Acts of 1945, 1946, and 1962 contained almost the same definition.[2] Only a relatively small sector of further education was concerned with systematic courses pitched above the GCE A level or the Ordinary National Certificate, that is with higher education in the strict sense.

Within a short space of time there has been a substantial increase in the financial support given to the higher education sector of further education, and a striking growth in the student population.[3]

There are two interrelated and much publicized reasons for the explosion of demand. The first reason is that in Britain, as in nearly all developed countries, we are being propelled towards a system of mass higher education, which the traditional universities are unable and do not wish to sustain. It has become widely accepted among parents and young people that without a degree or an equivalent qualification it is extremely difficult to take up a professional career. A degree may also confer social cachet. So an ever-rising proportion of young people are staying on at school beyond the compulsory leaving age and demanding the right to attend a post-school institution until they have obtained a professional qualification. The related reason for the expansion of higher education is that the government is obliged to face the consequences of its acceptance of the judgement of the Robbins Committee that higher education is a national necessity and of its own praiseworthy adherence to the principle that everyone merits an education appropriate to his intellectual capacity and willingness to learn.

To embrace an egalitarian principle is one thing, to deal satisfactorily with its financial implications is another. The logical step after the Robbins Committee had reported would have been simultaneously to expand the existing universities and to found more new ones of the Sussex or Lancaster type, but clearly the financial cost of such a development would have been astronomical and the government, embarrassed by an ailing economy, could not hope to meet it. Moreover, at that moment in time the government was also making the apparently unpalatable discovery that it was committed to university expansion yet had no guarantee that the universities would or could provide the categories and quantity of trained graduates that manpower forecasts indicated the economy would soon require. Besides, the universities were thought to spend money too lavishly. When he became Secretary of State for Education and Science, Anthony Crosland sought to escape from the dilemma by creating, or at least by postulating the idea of a, so-called, binary system, namely a system that would permit degree-granting higher education establishments, under strict governmental control, to exist alongside the universities.

Mr Crosland's assumption seemed to be that higher education institutions could conveniently be divided into two distinct groups: one group financed out of public funds through the Universities Grants Committee and enjoying a substantial degree of academic autonomy; the other offering mainly vocationally oriented courses and falling under the immediate control of the LEAs, except for a number of central institutions. Critics of the government suspected there had been a tacit decision to free the universities from the threat of increased interference, but in the future to give them fewer resources and to make them more cost conscious. Here was a calculated attempt both to cope with the unprecedented demand for higher education and to ensure the requisite flow of trained manpower for industry and commerce by investing more heavily than previously in the non-university sector, which the government could fashion according to its will and whose unit-costs would be much lower than those of the universities.[4]

If the government envisaged such a simple solution to the problem of demand, there was little chance of implementing it, for it was based upon an out-dated appraisal of the contemporary role of universities and ignored the essential unity of higher education, if not of tertiary education as a whole. Consider first the role of the universities. Their attention was far from being confined to 'pure' studies. Many of their courses had always been professionally based: medicine, law, and engineering, among other disciplines, are manifestly concerned with preparing undergraduates for specific careers. Other disciplines have of late shown themselves responsive to external social and economic pressures. Moreover, the UGC now pursues a policy of indicating which university departments should be allowed to expand and which to stand still or contract in the light of assumed national needs. Given the recent stress on public accountability and the assumption of responsibility for the oversight of universities by the Department of Education and Science, it is hard to see how the universities could be indifferent to governmental requirements even if they wished to ignore them – and there is, incidentally, no convincing evidence that they do.

The attempt to create two separate branches of higher education presupposes that the aims of education are divisible. This is evidently not so. Selective procedures can be used, of course, to classify students according to their intellectual ability – the best to Oxford and Cambridge, the next best to universities X and Y, and so on down a descending scale to local colleges of further education – but this does not absolve each institution from its obligation to provide students with the best possible learning environment; no institution is justified in using such shortcuts as inadequate library provision.

Discrimination between types of subjects is certainly not practicable, so that, for example, one set of universities might offer only 'pure' subjects and others only 'applied' subjects or one set might deal with liberal studies only and others with occupational courses only. In any event, there is abundant historical evidence that almost every higher education institution ends up by having a broad curriculum and by trying to compete with the standards of other institutions judged superior by society. Thus those Colleges of Advanced Technology that became universities have now established arts as well as social science faculties or schools. And who would venture to assert that the polytechnics will not in their turn also strive for ennoblement? The rational approach to the system of higher education is to treat it as a unified whole. Fortunately, this would appear to be the approach that is slowly being adopted despite Mr Crosland's foreshadowing of a bifurcated structure.

The problem of satisfying the demand for university education has been met by expanding the traditional universities, by establishing new universities, and by granting university charters to a number of Colleges of Advanced Technology. In the non-university sector, the other side of the binary system, the solution has been to adapt and enlarge existing further education institutions, to open a few new institutions, and to reform curricula and examination procedures. The result has been a spectacular but chaotic growth, made more complicated by the fact that professional associations and industrial and commercial firms now directly or indirectly sponsor institutions or course programmes that properly belong to the higher education sector, though they are independent of the universities. No description of the current pattern of higher education is complete without reference to such activities.

To chart the general expansion of the non-university sector would be an impossible task in a restricted compass.[5] The main developments may be reduced to the following: the expansion of polytechnics; new arrangements for the training of teachers;[6] the introduction of new academic awards; the proliferation of parttime courses; the founding of the Open University.

Perhaps the most remarkable innovation in the non-university sector of higher education has been the setting up of new polytechnics. The polytechnic idea is scarcely novel and indeed several polytechnics were established in London in the latter part of the nineteenth century and remain independent to this day. What is new is the government's determination to give them a key position in the expansion of higher education. Its intentions were set forth in a White Paper published in May 1966 with the title *A Plan for Polytechnics and other Colleges: Higher Education and the Further Education System*. Thirty colleges or groups of colleges with the generic title of polytechnics and located so as to ensure a representative geographical spread were to take on new functions. No more colleges were to be designated polytechnics for a period of ten years in order to allow the original thirty time for consolidation. By the academic session 1969–70 it was proposed that there should be a population of 70,000 students following sandwich as well as fulltime courses at degree and sub-degree level. Courses should be comprehensive in scope and character, and should enable students to study for first and higher degrees up to the same standards as in the universities. The staff would undertake research but their teaching duties would have first claim on their time. Close links would be forged with local industry and commerce and with the universities and colleges of education.

The distinguishing characteristics of a polytechnic are that it is primarily technologically based, serves a particular neighbourhood, is devoted primarily to teaching rather than research, is open to parttime students, is dependent on the services of parttime teachers, and is notably less autonomous than a university. In operation the polytechnics may turn out to be educationally mischievous. On the one hand they are likely to compete with and perhaps ape the universities. Already there are clear signs that the staff of polytechnics wish to stress their research function and to escape – rightly – from a technological straitjacket. They would also like to reduce their reliance on parttime staff. On the other hand they are likely to detract from the status and hence to lower the morale of other institutions in the further education field. During the last three years there have been cries of pain in the educational journals from the staff of colleges not among the select thirty, who obviously feel that they are being downgraded.

A necessary outcome of the appearance of the binary system has been the extension of higher academic awards, mainly through the creation by charter in 1964 of the Council for National Academic Awards (CNAA), a uniquely British institution. Prior to 1964 the only recourse of a student outside the universities who wished to take a degree was to register with the University of London for an external degree. The Robbins Committee, whose recommendations may well have had a greater impact on further education than on the universities, proposed that a national degree-granting body should be appointed to award degrees in the non-university sector. This proposal led to the formation of the CNAA and its absorption of the functions of the National Council for Technological Awards. The Council is empowered to award higher degrees, certificates, and diplomas as well as ordinary and honours first degrees. Individual colleges requiring recognition of a course submit to the Council details of the syllabus, the qualifications of the teaching staff, the type of accommodation in use, and the availability of teaching aids and essential equipment. The Council, which consists of representatives of teachers in further education, university staff, and industry and commerce, then decides whether or not to recognize the course. The machinery for dealing with requests for recognition is designed to ensure that CNAA degrees are comparable with those of the universities. A group of specialists visits the institution and subjects its teaching resources to a rigorous scrutiny. Courses are approved for a period of five years after which they must be reconsidered. Up to now the Council has attested to its concern for quality by rejecting most of the courses submitted for approval; the Education Section has so far not approved of a single education degree. Courses, which cover a wide spectrum of subjects, fall into four broad types, each supervised by a committee of the Council: science and technology; business studies; arts and social sciences; interdisciplinary studies.

In 1965 3,000 students were registered for CNAA awards; by 1969 the total had risen to 19,000, a small number compared to North America, for instance, but a noteworthy increase by British standards. A well-intentioned mechanism for breaching the degree-granting monopoly of the universities while ensuring the maintenance of satisfactory academic standards, the Council has predictably had to endure criticisms that it is catering for second-class citizens and debasing the currency of university degrees. Whereas initially the Council did seem to suffer from a sense of insecurity, it now shows signs of having acquired authority and external respect. The Committee of Vice-Chancellors has acknowledged the value of its work. Certainly there is a need for a central body to preside over the introduction to the non-university sector of degrees of a uniform academic standard. Moreover, because the institutions preparing students for CNAA degrees have close links with industry, the Council can justly claim that it is encouraging the development of indispensable courses.

Most of the courses coming under the aegis of the CNAA are 'sandwich courses', namely, day- or block-release courses. The hardships entailed in attending classes and studying solely in the evenings and at weekends are too familiar to need stressing; many students find regular evening attendance impossible, if only because of domestic ties. To overcome this handicap further education institutions are increasingly offering facilities for employed people to attend courses on one day a week or for long unbroken spells up to six months, so that periods of attendance are 'sandwiched' between periods of work. The staff of further education institutions resent any suggestion that courses are arranged on a day- or block-release basis simply to please employers and employees. On the contrary, they insist that there is invariably a fruitful interaction between study and work, and indeed that frequently the nature of the student's paid employment is such that it forms an integral part of his course – the application of theory and new skills in the practical work situation. Not surprisingly, before permitting their employees to study during working time, employers have to be persuaded that the firm stands to gain financially. There is accordingly an understandable tendency for employers to approve of work-release courses that will result in greater productivity, and to look askance at or to refuse support for all other courses. At the same time, a large number of employers now recognize that the pursuit of an academic award may make their employees more conscientious and more efficient when at work.

Besides those employees fortunate enough to attend day- or block-release courses there are tens of thousands of people in the UK, despite its limited geographical area, who wish to study for a higher academic award on a parttime basis, but who cannot do so for a variety of reasons, including a lack of facilities. Consideration of their needs by educationalists and government officials has led to proposals for the multiplication of parttime courses and in particular to the foundation of an open university. The case for extensive parttime higher education, long accepted in North America and the USSR, has still to be made out in the UK.

The main arguments in favour of parttime higher education in the UK context may be summarized as follows:

1 A significant percentage of the adult population did not attend a university, not because they lacked the academic ability but because they did not have the opportunity either through a shortage of money or because too few places were available when they applied for admission. A larger percentage of the population than was once realized are also late developers.

2 There will always be a minority of people who do not profit from formal education when young but who rise to positions of responsibility and power and then wish to further their education for social or professional reasons.

3 In the UK there is a bulge in the pre-adult population eligible for higher education which the existing institutions, stretched to capacity, cannot adequately accommodate.

4 So as to prosper a modern state must maximize the use of its manpower resources. It is not sufficient to train the coming generations for productive labour. Rather the present adult population must become immediately more productive through the raising of its level of educational attainment. There is a particularly acute national need for more people with scientific, technological, professional, and social skills.

5 Because of the accelerating rate at which knowledge expands, no one, not least a university graduate, can be prepared once and for all for a specialized career. Today's students leave school or university with little more than the rudiments of a subject at their command; much of what they are taught will soon be obsolescent. Frequent updating of their knowledge and improvement in their skills is imperative.

6 Some subjects, and certain aspects of subjects, are best studied in later life from the vantage point of experience and the insight gained through maturity.

7 The education of women has in general been neglected. On grounds of the wastage of potential talent as well as of social justice there is no longer any excuse for this neglect. The problem has two aspects. Many women were unable to proceed from school to university simply because of the attitude of society to their sex, whereas others were able to do so but found their careers cut short by early marriage and parenthood. Also, the value to society of having a large supply of educated women is at last being recognized, especially in such fields as teaching, nursing, and social work. Facilities are needed to enable mature

women to take first degree or similar courses and for women who already have a university qualification to return for a while to academic study so as to be able to resume their interrupted careers or to switch to new careers.

8 Not the least important argument in favour of parttime higher education is that teachers themselves in higher education often need to have points of contact with industry and commerce, and these may be found through teaching adults attending parttime courses.

9 Finally, the most compelling reason for advocating the expansion of parttime higher education is that it may well be a more efficient, as it is certainly a more economical, way of using national resources in support of public education. Fulltime education is uniformly costly throughout the world. Nevertheless, it is what students clamour for because they regard parttime courses as organized on the cheap, incompetently taught, and inferior in public esteem. For their part universities resist proposals to introduce or to extend parttime courses with the reasonable rejoinder that their resources, especially in teaching, are already overstretched. How can they staff yet more courses when they are hard pressed to cope with the current demand? Universities will surely not change their attitude unless they are compelled to do so by a government fiat or are persuaded that their academic standards will not suffer. What does seem certain is that if many more parttime degree and diploma courses were made available and if the universities were seen to be treating them seriously, then the prevailing demand for fulltime university places might slacken off.

There are at present two major obstacles to the spread of parttime courses. The first is the view of most educational institutions, especially the universities, that parttime courses should be of exactly the same standard as those taught internally. In four circumstances there is at least a case for offering parttime courses at a lower academic level than internal courses: 1 When the object is to raise to the appropriate standard the academic level of would-be candidates for admission by arranging pre-university entrance courses; 2 When an educational institution fills a gap that no other institution is able or willing to fill; 3 When an educational institution seeks to influence and to learn from non-graduates in responsible positions, such as trade union leaders; 4 When an educational institution decides that the best way to study a social need or problem is to make a practical experiment which may include providing teaching resources.

The second obstacle to the development of parttime courses is the inflexibility of the normal degree structure and the continuing undue reliance on formal examinations for the purpose of student assessment. Reform is indicated along the lines of the American practice of allowing students to accumulate credits which as a rule may be transferred from one institution to another. Such a reform would incidentally accord with research findings about the nature of the learning process.

Regardless of their present educational attainments it may be argued that adults should have an opportunity to find out for themselves whether they could benefit from university level courses. Good educational practice would seem to require that degree courses should be devised expressly for adults, and that methods of assessment should take into account their strength and weakness as learners – the fact, for instance, that adults perform less well than young people in written examinations completed against the clock.

These obstacles to the spread of parttime courses have largely been removed for students intending to embark on a degree course under the aegis of the Open University. Since the inauguration of this university is perhaps the most momentous of all the recent innovations in higher education, and since despite its nomenclature it belongs to the 'non-university' sector of the binary system, it is instructive to explain why it has been given a charter, how it is organized, and what functions it carries out.

In the beginning the main inspiration was egalitarian, namely, to make higher education widely accessible by founding a university that, while avowedly not poaching on the preserves of existing universities, would be open to all who could profit from its tuition. In the words of the *Report of the Planning Committee to the Secretary of State for Education and Science* (1969):

In summary, therefore, the objects of the Open University are to provide opportunities, at both undergraduate and postgraduate level, of higher education to all those who, for any reason, have been or are being precluded from achieving their aims through existing institutions of higher education. This does not imply competition with existing institutions, but rather an attempt on a national scale to complement their efforts; an attempt which may well increase the demands upon existing institutions, as students, stimulated by the experience of part-time study, increasingly come to want the opportunity for full-time study.

It would now appear, however, that the government can perceive the advantage of maintaining at least one university that can offer degree courses to a great mass of students at a reduced cost in staff and accommodation.

With the advent of the Open University it has become evident that we are in for a revolution in teaching methods. The most remarkable feature of the Open University is that it is using the multimedia system approach to teaching. Every night, with repeats on Saturday and Sunday mornings, it provides national broadcasts on television and radio by the British Broadcasting Corporation. Every student is given material to be studied by correspondence, written exercises to perform, and study kits where appropriate. There are prescribed texts for him to read and digest. He is also allocated a personal tutor, who marks his written work and generally tenders advice on his progress. Each tutor is responsible for supervising twenty students. Students spend one fortnight in residence each year on the campus of one of the universities, where they must undertake an intensive period of work inside and outside the classroom. In so far as possible facilities are provided for groups of students to assemble in selected study centres both to view the television programmes or to listen to the radio programmes and to engage in group discussion.

None of the methods being used is individually novel. What is innovative is the fact that they are being integrated systematically. Thus, whereas traditionally the main teaching input in universities has been through lectures, the emphasis here is upon stimulating the student to learn in a variety of ways. Significantly, although members of the academic staff decide what is to be taught, an applied educational methods unit is advising upon the various teaching methods that should be used, suggesting which parts can best be dealt with through the television medium, which parts through a correspondence course, and so on. The student follows a branching rather than a linear programme of study, so that when a gap in his knowledge or a failure to understand is exposed he can quickly be directed to remedial exercises. By making extensive use of computers the headquarters staff maintains a close watch on each student's progress.

The whole of the country has been divided up into regions, each under the supervision of a director, with supporting staff, who is responsible for arranging an interviewing and counselling service for would-be and for registered students, for selecting study centres, and for administering residential schools. In practice, counselling is carried out for the most part by parttime appointees, who are required to see students once a fortnight either singly or in groups. The appointment of counsellors is a significant departure since in the past parttime students were usually left to sink or swim unaided.

Students pay fees similar to those paid by fulltime students. These are not negligible in amount but certainly not so high as to deter a determined student, especially as LEAs may award bursaries at their discretion. Degrees are gained through accumulating credits, another overdue innovation in British practice. Academic standards are maintained by adopting the established practice of appointing external examiners from other universities to assist in preparing and marking examination papers.

As predicted by a market research survey, the Open University was initially overwhelmed by applications; the first year's cohort of students numbered 25,000. It is also being assumed that certain precautions being taken will guard against the catastrophic drop-out rate that has blighted so many previous adventures in parttime higher education. In short, the Open University bids fair to go a long way towards satisfying the pent-up demand for the mass provision of higher education. Its uniqueness lies in its nationwide remit, its liaison with the public broadcasting system, and its intention to exploit to the full all the teaching and learning aids produced by educational technology. Even if it proves to enjoy only a modified success, which becomes increasingly unlikely, it offers a way of coping with the explosive demand for higher education – a possible formula for dealing efficiently and economically with large numbers of students.

The non-university branch of the binary system is being used by the state not only as a means of producing certain types of trained manpower but also of preventing disaffection among those who cannot gain admission to the universities. The resulting expansion of resources has exposed the chaos that reigns in tertiary education as a whole, and this had led the Department of Education and Science and the Scottish Education Department, as well as the educational institutions themselves, to become aware of the need for rationalization.[7] Already it is being suggested that the polytechnics should be coordinated by the same body as the universities. To rationalize after a long period of unchecked and haphazard growth is, however, a formidable operation. It also raises a question of value. Just how accessible should higher education be? The Robbins Committee recommended that the system of higher education should be unified and that hierarchical divisions should be broken down. Opposition to the egalitarian mood of the 1960s is now palpably on the increase, and there are many who wish to see a return to the principle of elitism, not necessarily out of intellectual or social snobbery, but because they think that academic standards are falling and that the universities are losing their distinctive qualities. The elitist *versus* egalitarian controversy is exhaustively examined in other papers. It must suffice to end this paper by reiterating that whether it is desirable or not to introduce something like a three-tier system of tertiary education – and it probably is desirable – the idea of a binary system based on a supposed division of educational aims is untenable. The other side of the binary system will suffer if it is treated as a crude instrument for producing trained manpower on the cheap.

NOTES

[1] Strictly speaking 'further education' includes 'adult education'; in practice, the two are distinguished.

[2] In a paper of this sort one is faced with the difficulty that there are important differences between the educational systems of Scotland on the one hand, and England and Wales on the other. Most of the statements contained herein apply equally to both systems; some relate only to England and Wales.

[3] The numbers enrolled in higher education during the session 1969–70 were: universities 219,500; colleges of education 118,400; advanced further education 90,000.

[4] The government appears to believe that the operational costs of the universities, polytechnics and colleges of education are in the ratio of 5:4:3 respectively.

[5] The role of the central institutions in Scotland, for instance, requires special consideration. Neither is it possible here to deal with Schools and Colleges of Art and Colleges of Music.

[6] This topic will not be considered here since it is dealt with in another paper.

[7] Before and after demitting office Mr Edward Short, the last minister to be responsible for education under the labour government, stated that the binary system must go. In his view it had been introduced as the first step in rationalizing the whole field of tertiary education.

REFERENCE

Report of the Planning Committee to the Secretary of State for Education and Science. 1969: London: HMSO.

RECOMMENDED READING

BRATCHELL, D. F. 1968. *The Aims and Organisation of Further Education*. London: Pergamon.

CANTOR, L., and ROBERTS, F. 1969. *Further Education in England and Wales*. London: Routledge and Kegan Paul.

PETERS, A. J. 1967. *British Further Education: A Critical Textbook*. London: Pergamon.

ROBINSON, E. 1968. *The New Polytechnics*. London: Cornmarket Press and Penguin Books.

Types of higher education: comprehensive, coordinated, or classified*

J. STEVEN WATSON

Any discussion of types of higher education in the 1970s must be conducted under pressure. The pressure is that of numbers. The discussants will be politicians and parents as well as professors.

The growth in the amount of higher education is, of course, a feature of a growing technological society. In the United States the Department of Health, Education, and Welfare reported that 72 per cent of those in elementary education in 1960 were completing secondary education successfully in 1967; more than half of these, that is 40 per cent of the elementary class, then entered into higher education. In the USSR (statistics produced in Paris) the figures are comparable with those of the USA; there is a student population of five million in higher education, or some $2\frac{1}{2}$ per cent of the total population. Both these great powers practise selective entry to higher education. France, with unselective entry (that is, the right of all holders of the certificate for successful completion of secondary education to enter into higher education), has yet a smaller percentage of its youth in higher education. Somewhere between 20 per cent and 25 per cent of the appropriate age-group in the autumn of 1968 were qualified for their entry upon the next stage.

In France, as in Britain, the direction of movement is more important for our discussion than the absolute numbers or existing percentages. 'En l'espace de vingt ans l'action conjugé de la demographie, de l'augmentation de taux de scolarisation dans les enseignement élémentaire et secondaire du développement économique au multiplié par 20 le stock d'etudiants' (Casadevail 1970). In Britain the projections constructed by the Department of Education and Science suggest that the same factors of extended secondary education and so on will entail a doubling of the numbers in higher education over the next decade. This should probably be regarded as a minimum programme. But the matter of its cost immediately provokes questions about the proper type, both in duration and content, of this expanding higher education; it may also stimulate discussion of whether this expansion is related to increased possibilities of wealth, whether higher education is, so to speak, to pay for its own improvement by a growth in the GNP.

I am not disposed to argue the case for higher education in terms of consequential increases in wealth. It is enough, I think, to face the fact that a society as it grows more technologically advanced demands more higher education. There are two obvious ways in which this is true. There is first the obvious need for a large part of the population to be resourceful and able to use the tools of a sophisticated world. There is also – and I regard this as just as important – the desire of men and women to have part of the dividend paid to them in the form of a richer cultural life, as well as in leisure and material goods. A richer cultural life does not mean simply an ability to understand art exhibitions or the theatre; it should include the pleasures of numeracy, an ability to understand and live happily with a computer society. Thus, there are vocational and social reasons that make the expansion of higher education inevitable all over the developed world.

Once higher numbers are accepted the question must be asked as to whether the style of higher education must remain the same as it increases in quantity. Should the institutions in which the young receive their training reflect the two reasons, vocational and cultural, for the increase in higher education? Does more mean not worse but different, different at least in balance? Then, if there are different types of higher educational institution, how should each section select its entrants? Should a *numerus clausus* operate based upon public needs?

In the United States the first result of wider sharing of higher education was to swell universities to sizes that have made student unrest inevitable. But even the swollen universities could not cope with higher numbers. However, the growth of what are now called community colleges, institutions giving academic (liberal arts) as well as vocational training for periods shorter than a full university course, has been striking in the last decade. Six-hundred thousand were enrolled in the two-year community colleges in 1960; in 1970 two million. The plan now is to have four million enrolled in 1980. These are classified as teaching institutions. 'Teachers are there because they like to teach,' says Mr Henderson, the Director of the Florida Department of Education (as quoted in the *New York Times*). 'That's their goal. They're not researching. They are not publishing. They are teaching.'

This higher education institution is coordinated to some extent with the full universities. A student who is good enough, judged by the college board psychological and other tests, may go directly to a first- or second- or third-class university. One who fails to make this grade may get to the community college, and will live at home and commute. The college is comprehensive in that it will include most academic disciplines and perhaps some thirty-six vocational courses from truck-driving to accountancy. But there is a ladder of promotion for the academically minded to get into the university proper after a preliminary period in the community college. About two-thirds of the entrants, according to Dr Chapman of Cuyahoga Community College, Ohio (*New York Times*), have the ambition to use this training as a means of getting a second chance at the university. About 50 per cent of these, or one-third of the entry, do go on to the university, joining, two years later, their school-fellows who went straight in. The advantage claimed for this system is that it allows a double selection, that it is a cheap form of spreading some form of higher instruction, and that it caters for those, particularly those from poor homes, whose chief desire is a quick ticket to a better job.

The West German rectors' conference is at present proposing a more egalitarian and, in my opinion, less realistic scheme for dealing with the problems of expanding numbers and hence of selection. On their plan the existing universities, technical colleges, and so on, of West Germany would be regrouped so as to produce truly comprehensive universities. It is comparable to the process of setting up comprehensive schools in Britain's secondary education system. The old university would absorb the other higher institutions. All possessors of the school-leaving diploma would be entitled to enter and then to decide their courses, vocational or academic or mixed, with the advice of the university staff. All the staff, whether from the technical side or from the purest academic background, whether a Nobel prize winner in physics or an efficient instructor in pedagogics, would have the same rights to pursue research as well as teach.

Such all-purpose institutions would, of course, be even more regional than the existing universities. They would also have to be large institutions, in British if not in American eyes, with student bodies as large as 20,000. It is argued that they would avoid the errors of an eighteen-plus selection by allowing for continuous changing between streams right up to graduation. This would also diminish the snobbery between different branches of higher education.

In Britain, we must admit, such snobbery is widely prevalent. It has, if anything, been increased by the promotion of some former colleges of technology to university status, and the declaration of a binary system. Though the polytechnics and teacher-training colleges are making progress towards greater participation by their staff in their own government, it is clear that the original intention was to separate self-governing, researching, universities from publicly controlled vocational teaching institutions. The UCCA entry system has, within the universities sector, tended to emphasize inequality of status to the point where attempts can be made to write down a pecking order and to ask for a table that will show the exact difficulty of entry for intending candidates.

If Germany is planning to be comprehensive, if the United States is coordinated, we in Britain have now a system of classified higher education. What is the basis of this classification, what effects will larger numbers have upon it and upon entry-selection, and will it allow sufficient flexibility to provide the requirements, cultural and vocational, for the future? If we retain the binary division should we expect the share of new entrants to be divided fifty-fifty between the two sides? Is it cheaper for the non-autonomous sector to expand than for the universities? Can we regulate growth in the light of probable industrial need, or should we follow the desires of the students? Within the university sector do we accept the doctrine of centres of excellence? How far is it necessary to develop residence as a part of university life?

I have put down only a few of the questions that arise, and I will certainly not attempt answers to all of these, but I think we may begin by considering 'what is a university?' Let us at the outset reject an idea, based upon the distinction between vocational and cultural needs which I earlier mentioned, that universities are necessarily pure academic institutions without any interest in practical training. The medieval university prepared men for careers in medicine, the law, the church, and public affairs at the same time as they discussed the fundamental philosophical problems about man's place in the universe. Modern technology has a corpus of knowledge and raises a range of questions that certainly make it suitable as a university discipline; so here the universities can again combine their search for knowledge with sound vocational training.

This suggests, however, the beginning of a definition of the role of the university within the system of higher education. At each stage of the educational pattern, from infant schools up through post-experience refresher courses, two elements are involved, the transmission of facts and the questioning of accepted knowledge. At the earlier stages, however, the instructor is more concerned with passing on past experience than in questioning the fruits of this experience himself or in encouraging others to question it. The more advanced the teaching, the greater the element of questioning ought to be. Questioning means, when we get to higher education, the combination of research with teaching. The more theoretical the subject the more the emphasis needs to be upon discovery, and the less it is upon know-how.

If, therefore, I were called on to define a university it would be as the major institution in which past experience is transmitted while at the same time it is tested and new knowledge is discovered. Some independent investigation will no doubt improve the quality of man's teaching of hotel management, but it will be essential to the teaching, at university level, of theoretical physics. Not all teachers, despite the West German rectors, are equally drawn to research or capable of it. On the other hand, the teaching from which all research is rigorously excluded, as in the American community colleges, is hardly higher education at all, it is more like secondary education for the older man or woman. But my point is that the university in its transmission of knowledge, whether the knowledge has vocational use or not, is bound at the same time to question and explore the bases upon which accepted opinion rests. Let me say at once therefore that it should be a cause of concern in Scotland that its universities have been less favoured in this respect than some in England. But in stressing research one should not go so far as to make a university into a research institute. The teaching function of a university is important not only to the nation but to the researcher. The same man should be involved in the exploration of and the reporting to his pupils of the significance of his work and its relationship to the wider field. In consequence the university will be an expensive form of higher education, because classes will have to be small to permit the sort of intimate explanation and discussion involved in this relationship. For this reason, while I welcome the greater use of audio-visual aids for economizing in valuable time spent in passing on information, I also fear their misuse if this lessens the intimacy of the most important part of university teaching.

Another element in my concept of a university is the requirement for the institution not to be too narrowly specialized. But this point leads on to the range of subjects discussed elsewhere in this volume. Suffice it then to note that there may be some specialization but nevertheless to be a university an institution must cover more than just technologies or liberal arts. The spread over science, arts, and social studies must be maintained for the very practical reason that it will attract talented students.

A further reason is that, in my view, ideally a university should be a community or a federation of communities. In the exploration of new ideas the points of growth are often on the border lines between disciplines. In the Scottish system, of allowing pupils to feel their way towards specialization as they proceed, it is very necessary to bring students into intellectual contact with a wide variety of the activities going on in the institution (and I prefer this system to instant decisions made immediately on entry to university). It is not enough to break up a large body into units each grouped round its own subject; it is desirable to allow both staff and students to associate with those who have interests different from their own. I believe this is most easily done in a residential university, and my own experience in St Andrews and at Oxford comes to mind here. At the moment this fourth element in the make-up of a university, its community life, is not given much prominence in Europe. However, I remain convinced of its value.

In indicating the elements that combine to form a university I would not wish to deny that they may be found mixed in different proportions in a given institution; nor would I deny that these same features may be found in institutions that are not universities. At the moment the direction of trends in England is that a poly-technic may encourage its staff to undertake fundamental research, it may provide correspondingly expensive teaching methods, and it may rebuild itself on a big new community campus where new subjects are added to its curriculum. All one can say then is that any such institution is becoming a university in fact, whatever label one sticks on it. Indeed, in the spectrum of higher education it is a matter of taste, or government policy, where one draws the line between universities and other institutions.

One reason, apart from snobbery, for drawing that line is financial policy. If it is accepted that a true university-type education is expensive, and if attempts are then made to prevent other forms of higher education from increasing this expensive 'university element' in what they offer, then methods of selecting students for the expensive privilege of university education becomes more important than ever. Yet we know that all our selection procedures are suspect.

In this context ideas of two-year courses become relevant. In the House of Lords Professor Lord Tedder advanced a scheme that clearly owes something to United States experience. He proposed the admission of all students into institutions that would give a two-year course ending in a degree of BA or the equivalent, which we can call stage A. The best of these stage A graduates would then go on to take a further two years for an MA or the equivalent in another institution, stage B. Finally, a percentage of these students would be allowed to go on further still for a doctorate or diploma in advanced work in a third institution, stage C. The advantages claimed for this proposal are that it allows for a more efficient selection of students to take up long and expensive courses; at the same time it gives a recognized label to many who want some higher education but would be unwilling to spend more time than necessary in acquiring it. There can be no doubt that in Lord Tedder's mind the older residential universities, St Andrews in particular, would be most appropriately concerned with the graduate work in stage C, and the more sprawling urban centres would be more appropriate to stage A.

My own first comment was that I would like at the least an overlap of A with B and of B with C in order to preserve both standards and a reasonably mixed community. On further consideration I agree that we may be forced to a solution of this sort, but I prefer to maintain as long as possible our mix of senior and junior students in any given institution as well as our wide range of institutions. I am already worried by the greater concentration of resources being carried out by the Science Research Council; I fear this leads to a rigidity in the credit-ratings of institutions, which is good neither for them nor for the advancement of knowledge, since the latter is likely to be a ragged advance in which it is not always the biggest battalions or the most skilled people who take the decisive step forward.

I hope we will preserve some flexibility in our higher education system, that we will continue to be aware of the difference between university and other forms of education, but that it will be possible to have institutions moving up or down in public esteem. But if we are to have a continuation of the existing rather unorganized system it is clear that we must also improve relations between different sectors of the system. Students should be able more easily, and without a sense of failure, to move from one area of higher education to another, as experience shows they would profit by such a move. There should be closer contacts between the institutions themselves. I personally would like to see a university taking a share in all other higher education locally. Lord Annan, who has called this the umbrella system, believes that other institutions fear the big-brother approach of universities, and would reject them. He may be right – perhaps Elmwood, Cupar, would not wish St Andrews to adopt a paternal attitude towards them. Nevertheless, in some way or other, at least in big urban areas, we should contrive more dialogue and cooperation in the use of resources by our various forms of higher education. But I would no more welcome the comprehensive German system than the classified American one.

More questions have been raised here than answers provided. If the rather untidy British system continues over the next decade it looks probable that the non-autonomous sector will grow faster than the university sector in numbers of students. I would hope that it would also grow in prestige. But the university will remain at the top of the system because it exists to combine research with instruction. It is my belief also that the older residential universities will be able to appeal to a numerically small but particularly able section of young men and women. They will continue to provide a valuable element in this mixed pattern of higher education. The argument for a good supply of funds to them is an extreme form of the argument of all universities; what they do is admittedly expensive but the article they produce is distinctive and necessary.

NOTE

* This paper was, of course, written before the publication of the White Paper on the next ten years of educational development.

REFERENCES

CASADEVAIL, A. F. 1970. Unpublished paper presented to European Rector's Conference, November 1970, Vienna.

Hansard. 1970. Lord Tedder's Speech in the House of Lords. Recorded in Hansard No. 767, House of Lords; Weekly Hansard Vol. 311, 14–16 July 1970, p. 672.

New York Times. 28 November 1970, p. 23.

A postgraduate revolution?*

J. N. WOLFE

The system of higher education in Great Britain is undergoing very rapid and far-reaching changes at the present time. The aim of this paper is to examine some special aspects of that development. It is concerned, in particular, with the role that research and postgraduate study are beginning to play in that system.

The system of higher education is conceived of as having three principal outputs: students with undergraduate degrees; students with postgraduate degrees; and research. The most striking change in the present period in comparison with that before the war is the growth in importance of the output of students with postgraduate degrees. One aim of this paper is to examine the way in which this growth has been distributed among the different universities, and to examine the implications of the emerging pattern.

The growth of higher education in Great Britain is acknowledged to be one of the most striking features of this century. What is equally striking, if sometimes less noticed, is the growth of postgraduate education. The expansion in postgraduate studies in the UK can be seen in *Table 1*, which shows the number of postgraduate students and undergraduate students enrolled for fulltime study at universities in 1939, 1951, 1955, and 1968. It will be seen that while the undergraduate population has risen roughly fourfold in the twenty-nine years covered, the postgraduate population has risen nearly thirteenfold (*Table 1*).

Table 2 shows the change in the proportion of postgraduates in relation to total fulltime university enrolment on the same basis for different years. It will be seen that the major shift occurred in the immediately postwar period. It will be noticed, however, that this

TABLE 1 Postgraduate and undergraduate students engaged in fulltime study in universities in Great Britain

Year	Postgraduates	Undergraduates
1939	3021	38508
1951	11327	67843
1955	12668	72526
1968	37994	173528

proportion has continued to grow fairly steadily from 1957 in spite of the check occasioned by the differential increase in fees for overseas students late in the period. A continuation of the recent trend would suggest that postgraduate enrolment would approach 22 per cent of total university enrolment by 1981.

Since about three-quarters of all postgraduate students are British, and since the average duration of fulltime postgraduate training is less than that for undergraduate training, this figure would indicate that a very substantial proportion of the graduates from British universities now undergo some form of postgraduate

TABLE 2 The proportion of postgraduate students to all fulltime students

Year	Postgraduates as a percentage of total number of university students
1931	5·9
1939	7·3
1951	14·3
1953	14·6
1955	14·6
1957	14·7
1959	16·0
1961	17·1
1963	17·8
1965	16·9
1967	17·5
1968	18·0

training. It seems reasonable to assume that up to two-thirds of those with first-class or upper second-class qualifications now take such training. The emergence of a pattern of higher education in which postgraduate training is a normal part of the educational experience of the more talented graduate is likely to have profound effects on the undergraduate curriculum. There is already considerable pressure, particularly from industry, for a diminution in the degree of specialization in undergraduate courses. As postgraduate training increases in popularity the movement towards greater breadth in the undergraduate programme is likely to gain strength.

It is everywhere accepted that research and postgraduate training are highly complementary. It is, however, no longer universally acknowledged that there needs to be a close connection between research and undergraduate training. In the Soviet Union there appears to have been a conscious attempt to separate research and postgraduate training from the universities and to place them in separate institutions. The apparent uniformity of the American university system conceals a substantial degree of specialization. A large portion of the American higher education system operates with a minimal background of research activity, and while few institutions devoted exclusively to research and postgraduate study have emerged in the United States, there has been a tendency for PhD students to become concentrated in the hands of twenty or thirty universities of great renown.

It has, for a long time, been widely accepted in the UK that high quality undergraduate teaching requires a background of research in the same institution as a means of ensuring that teaching is kept fresh and modern. This doctrine is not always pressed so far as to insist that all university teachers should actively engage in research. Nor is the stimulating effect of postgraduate teaching and the presence of postgraduate students always accepted. There is no general agreement, moreover, on how intense the preoccupation with research needs to be in order to produce an optional teaching programme, and in some institutions a very limited volume of research is certainly thought to be sufficient. Perhaps partly because of this there has been very little opposition in academic circles to the proliferation and expansion of institutions of higher education like the polytechnics, which have little explicit commitment to the idea of research. This non-research oriented sector of higher education may soon be able to produce students with undergraduate degrees at substantially lower cost than the universities, and so seems likely to become an increasingly important competitor to the universities.

There exists, moreover, a substantial measure of concentration of research and postgraduate training within the universities of Britain. A large part of total Research Council support has gone to a small number of institutions. The dispersion of postgraduate students among the universities is also highly skewed. There is some apparent tendency for the concentration of postgraduate studies in a few institutions. Oxford and Cambridge, for example, are approaching a 25 per cent postgraduate enrolment, and the University of London 28 per cent. It does not appear, however, that any university institutions totally devoted to postgraduate training will emerge in the UK within the foreseeable future.

The skewness of the distribution of postgraduate enrolment is paralleled by the skewness in the distribution of PhDs awarded. In the postwar period there has been a surprising constancy in the degree of skewness of these distributions. Moreover, the analysis of the determinants of future trends suggests that the relatively small recent change in the degree of skewness is likely to be reversed in the future. These points are discussed in detail in the Appendix to which the attention of the reader is directed.

The apparent stability of the degree of skewness of the distribution of postgraduate enrolment among British universities is, however, very misleading in some respects. This stability conceals the changing fortunes of individual institutions. More importantly, however, it conceals the considerable decline in the dominance of a few institutions in postgraduate studies. The position emerges fairly clearly from *Table 3* which shows the proportion of total postgraduate enrolment accounted for by the enrolment of specific institutions in 1955 and 1968.

Table 4 shows the league table of university institutions by number of fulltime postgraduates enrolled in 1955 and 1968. *Table 5* shows the proportion of postgraduate students in each institution in those two years. *Table 6* indicates the change in the number of postgraduates in each institution between 1955 and 1968. *Table 7* gives an indication of the change in the proportion of postgraduates to total enrolment between these two years.

Table 8a shows the distribution, by university, of PhDs awarded as well as the ratio of PhDs awarded to postgraduate enrolment.

TABLE 3 The proportion of all fulltime postgraduates in Great Britain studying in institutions concentrating on postgraduate study, 1955 and 1968

	1955		*1968*	
University	*% of all GB postgraduates*	*University*	*% of all GB postgraduates*	
London	32·3	London	25·4	
Cambridge	8·9	Oxford	7·6	
Oxford	8·4	Cambridge	6·5	
Edinburgh	5·3	Birmingham	4·7	
Birmingham	4·4	Manchester	3·9	
Manchester	4·1	Leeds	3·8	
Durham	3·7	Liverpool	3·5	
Leeds	3·7	Edinburgh	3·5	
Glasgow	3·4	Nottingham	2·9	
Liverpool	3·2	Bristol	2·7	
(38% of all universities)	77·5	(24% of all universities)	64·5	

NOTE: Durham University is later split into Durham and Newcastle

This ratio would seem to be a tolerably good indication of the extent to which postgraduates in each university have been concentrated upon courses having a high research content.

The distribution of postgraduate students from overseas among universities is given in *Table 8b*. It will be seen that there is a noticeable variation around the average figure of 25 per cent overseas enrolment. Oxford and London have a particularly high percentage of overseas enrolment.

It will be seen from these tables that the distribution of postgraduates is becoming more evenly spread among the larger institutions. This trend seems likely to accelerate in the future. Nevertheless, many universities are still almost entirely undergraduate in character. It appears therefore that the system of higher education is moving towards a situation in which a group of a dozen or so universities will have a substantial, but not exclusive, interest in postgraduate studies and in which the rest of the institutions of

TABLE 4 Institutions concentrating on postgraduate study in 1955 and 1968: Numbers of fulltime postgraduates

1955		1968	
University	Number of postgraduates	University	Number of postgraduates
London	4096	London	8372
Cambridge	1129	Oxford	2519
Oxford	1064	Cambridge	2151
Edinburgh	673	Birmingham	1537
Birmingham	561	Manchester	1271
Manchester	524	Leeds	1262
Durham	469	Liverpool	1166
Leeds	467	Edinburgh	1144
Glasgow	432	Nottingham	942
Liverpool	405	Bristol	896

NOTE: Durham University is later split into Durham and Newcastle.

TABLE 5 Institutions concentrating on postgraduate study in 1955 and 1968: Proportion of postgraduates in the total student body

1955		1968	
University	Number of Postgraduates % of all fulltime Students	University	Number of Postgraduates % of all fulltime Students
London	24	London	28
Birmingham	18	Birmingham	24
Leeds	16	Oxford	23
Oxford	15	Nottingham	21
Edinburgh	15	Cambridge	21
Liverpool	15	Liverpool	18
Manchester	15	Manchester	17
Nottingham	14	Leeds	16
Cambridge	14	Bristol	16
Bristol	13	Edinburgh	13

TABLE 6 Institutions concentrating on postgraduate study in Great Britain: changes in the numbers of postgraduates from 1955 to 1968

University	Index 1968 (1955 = 100)
Nottingham	349
Liverpool	288
Birmingham	274
Leeds	270
Bristol	264
Manchester	243
Oxford	237
London	204
Cambridge	191
Edinburgh	170
Glasgow	154

TABLE 7 Institutions concentrating on postgraduate study in 1955 and 1968: changes in the proportion of postgraduates in the total student body

University	Index 1968 (1955 = 100)
Oxford	153
Cambridge	150
Nottingham	150
Birmingham	133
Bristol	123
Liverpool	120
London	116
Manchester	113
Leeds	100
Glasgow	100
Edinburgh	87

TABLE 8a   Distribution of doctorates awarded in 1967 in the top twelve doctorate-awarding universities

	Doctorates awarded	Number of doctorates as % of all postgraduate students
	1967	1967
London	961	11·5
Cambridge	426	19·8
Oxford	282	11·2
Birmingham	204	13·3
Leeds	179	14·2
Manchester	154	12·1
Liverpool	136	11·7
Glasgow	131	19·7
Edinburgh	128	11·2
Manchester Institute of Science and Technology	128	17·5
Sheffield	127	15·3
Nottingham	103	10·9

higher education, including the polytechnics, will emerge as a continuing chain showing a progressively increasing concentration on undergraduate studies.

It may be asked whether such a development would provide for the most efficient utilization of academic resources within the UK. Should research and postgraduate work be spread so widely among the universities? And should so large a proportion of the higher education system be left without any substantial research base? In practice, however, the present tendencies may be inevitable in view of the scarcity of high quality academic talent, the stringency of funds in a rapidly growing higher education sector, and the desire of university staff to be allowed to pursue their research interests. The practical issues may lie in quite different directions: on the provision of frequent sabbatical leaves for research for staff in institutions not highly favoured by research funds or postgraduate students; in the development of a few high quality institutions devoted entirely to postgraduate study and research; and in the

TABLE 8b   Distribution of postgraduates from overseas

University	*Number of overseas postgraduates*	*Total number of postgraduates*	*Number of overseas postgraduates/ total number of postgraduates* %
London	3274	8372	39·1
Oxford	740	2519	29·4
Birmingham	363	1537	23·6
Cambridge	518	2151	24·1
Manchester Institute of Science and Technology	238	732	32·5
Leeds	289	1262	22·9
Southampton	166	753	22·0
Liverpool	179	1166	15·4
Nottingham	136	942	14·4
Reading	203	771	26·3
Manchester	294	1271	23·1
Sheffield	126	831	15·2
Bristol	145	896	16·2
Edinburgh	299	1144	26·1
Glasgow	134	665	20·2

(1968)

NOTE:

1 This table shows the numbers of overseas students included in each of the major universities both separately and as a percentage of the total postgraduate enrolment. It will be seen that Edinburgh is not markedly different from other universities in its percentage of overseas postgraduates, although Oxford and London have an exceptionally high proportion of overseas postgraduate students.

2 The position of Edinburgh and the Scottish universities generally should be considered in the context of the changing role of three-year and four-year undergraduate degrees in these institutions. In so far as Scottish universities retain a four-year honours degree the size of their graduating honours classes is smaller relatively to their total enrolment than is the case in English universities. Moreover the total undergraduate teaching load may be larger in relation to the total undergraduate population.

recognition that appointment and promotion in the most favoured institutions will have to be increasingly based on research productivity.

APPENDIX

S. N. Brissimis

The purpose of this appendix to the main article is to apply the probabilistic Markov chain approach to the study of the concentration of fulltime postgraduate students in a small number of universities in Great Britain. This method has had many fruitful applications in economics but it must be pointed out that it does not offer any insight into the forces underlying a particular process. A cloak variable takes on the task of describing the pattern of change that can be ascribed to these forces. This variable will be for us the share that universities in Great Britain have in the postgraduate population. We assume that they are grouped according to this criterion in five classes. The data for the years 1955 and 1968 are tabulated in *Table A*.

TABLE A

Class intervals %	1955		1968	
	% of all universities	% of all postgraduates	% of all universities	% of all postgraduates
0–1	17	2	37	7
1–2	38	15	28	18
2–3	14	9	14	14
3–5	17	19	14	22
5–100	14	55	7	39
	100	100	100	100

Since no movement could be detected in successive years because of the small number of class intervals taken, the transitional probabilities have been computed for the above two years. The implicit assumption in this case is that these probabilities remain invariant throughout the evolutionary process. Provision has also been made for entry of new universities and departure of existing ones; the latter, however, need not mean the closing down of these universities but simply merging of available statistical data. The first row and first column in the transition matrix account for these facts.

The probabilities were approximated by pertinent relative frequencies and the indeterminacy in the number of potential entrants into the system was solved by taking their number to be 100, an arbitrary selection.

The matrix actually obtained was used to determine the equilibrium distribution of postgraduates from the simultaneous system of equations:

$$[x_0 \; x_1 \; x_2 \; x_3 \; x_4 \; x_5] \begin{bmatrix} 0.84 & 0.13 & 0.01 & 0.02 & 0 & 0 \\ 0.2 & 0.4 & 0.4 & 0 & 0 & 0 \\ 0 & 0.09 & 0.73 & 0.18 & 0 & 0 \\ 0.25 & 0 & 0 & 0.5 & 0.25 & 0 \\ 0 & 0 & 0.2 & 0 & 0.6 & 0.2 \\ 0 & 0 & 0 & 0 & 0.25 & 0.75 \end{bmatrix}$$
$$= [x_0 \; x_1 \; x_2 \; x_3 \; x_4 \; x_5] \quad (1)$$

$x_0 =$ the proportion of potential entrants to the system
$x_1 =$ the proportion of universities whose share is between 0 and 1 and so on.

Dropping out one of the six equations above which can be shown to be linearly dependent on the others and taking into account that the elements of the probability vector $[x_0 \; x_1 \; x_2 \; x_3 \; x_4 \; x_5]$ must sum to unity, the solution is easily taken as

$$[0.29325 \quad 0.10263 \quad 0.26064 \quad 0.10555 \quad 0.13193 \quad 0.10555]. \quad (2)$$

But since our choice of the potential entrants was completely arbitrary it is more appropriate to delete the first element and

TABLE B

Class intervals %	Equilibrium % of all universities
0–1	15
1–2	37
2–3	15
3–5	18
5–100	15
	100

normalize the remaining so that $\sum_{i=1}^{5} x_i = 1$. The results are shown in *Table B*.

What is immediately evident from the above table is that the equilibrium distribution is not much different from that in 1955.

The next step is to compute the Gini coefficient, a well-known measure of concentration, form the data of *Tables A* and *B*. The formulae

$$g = \frac{d}{2\mu} \tag{3}$$

$$d = \frac{2}{N^2} \sum_{i=1}^{5} (N - Q_i) Q_i (X_{i+1} - X_i) \tag{4}$$

are used where g = the Gini coefficient, μ the mean share, Q_i the cumulative percentage of universities, X_i the central value of the i-th class interval and N the sum of simple percentages of universities. The coefficients for 1955, 1968 and equilibrium were 36·2 per cent, 37·3 per cent and 35·9 per cent respectively. The uniformity in computations of the three coefficients permits us at least to trace correctly their movement. A small increase is present in 1968 compared to 1955. A reasonable explanation for this could be looked for in that newly created universities start off with low percentages of postgraduates. Therefore, although a decrease in the individual shares of particular universities is to be expected, the net result is a rise in the overall degree of concentration. The situation in the future, however, will be different; the results of the application of Markov chain analysis to the evolution of the system indicate the restoration of the previous status.

Nevertheless, a grouping of data using more detailed class intervals would certainly reveal movements not perceptible under the broad grouping attempted here. Moreover, averaging out the transition matrices' elements over a number of successive years could strengthen the conclusions reached.

ACKNOWLEDGEMENT

   * I would like to acknowledge useful discussion on this topic with my colleagues, Professors I. G. Stewart and A. J. Youngson, and with Principal Michael Swann. The calculations on which this paper is based were carried out by Miss A. Mackney.

Universities and the enemies of excellence

MAX BELOFF

In discussing the theory and measurement of academic quality in the preceding essay Professor Wolfe has assumed that what we mean by academic excellence is related to one important function of a university, that of advancing knowledge through research, and has suggested that, on this assumption, there does exist some possibility at least of making objective comparisons between one university and another. I would not myself wish to disparage this approach, nor to deny the importance of research and publication in the university spectrum, but it is an approach that may seem more obvious and even axiomatic to a natural scientist or to a social scientist: to someone concerned with the applied sciences, and even more to someone like myself who is no scientist at all, other functions of a university may seem to bulk equally large. These other functions are at least two in number: teaching, and especially undergraduate teaching, that is to say the training of young people, the majority of whom will not pursue an academic or scientific career; and a less definable function which I would call that of maintaining cultural standards in the quality of the university's own life, and not least in its extracurricular activities whether supported by staff, students, or both.

In all these respects a university that was, by my definition, a centre of excellence or even was trying to be one would be very unlike the kind of university that appears to be becoming the norm, in the western world at least. The more I have considered universities and their problems during the last few troubled years, the more I have become aware of how difficult and artificial an institution a real university must be, and of the extent to which its values must not only be different from those of society at large but even opposed to those values profoundly.

When I have tried to explain it, I have usually found myself up against the accusation that what I am proposing is essentially reactionary; and, indeed, in the literal meaning of that much abused word it is true, since these ideas are indeed the product of a reaction to what is going on in our universities and in American universities whose downward path our university authorities seem determined to follow as rapidly as may be. But I would not even be very worried if this was meant in the most common-sense meaning of the word 'reactionary', that is backward looking. For I think that in some respects our universities were on a more rewarding track up till about a quarter of a century ago.

It does for instance involve the view that the transmission of the knowledge and wisdom of the past is more important, even in a rapidly changing world, than adding to that knowledge, and indeed that one of the main functions of a university is to act as a constant reminder of how insignificant are the advances we have made in all but pure science and technology compared with the major differences that exist between civilized and non-civilized societies; and of how, substantially, the social and political and philosophical problems that confront man in society are permanent, and in a sense forever in their entirety insoluble. A university that believes (in any sense but the technological and instrumental) that its business is to be 'relevant' is no university at all.

Similarly, such views involve an unfashionable accent on the being of an academic community as opposed to its product, whether that product be measured in terms of degrees awarded or of research carried out and published. They involve accepting that a community of this kind, dedicated to the pursuit of learning in a particular way through the appropriate methods of the several disciplines, is bound to appeal to relatively few men and women as the right way of life for them – even people with strong intellectual interests may be better advised to pursue them in quite different kinds of institutions, research organizations for instance – and not by any means to all intelligent young people as producing the atmosphere they most require in the heady years of adolescence and early adulthood.

Furthermore, because the whole set of ideas upon which a university must rest is a very complex one, and because what it needs to make it work successfully are not merely the correct rules but also the correct conventions of behaviour – dictated as they should be by respect for the learning and experience of the teacher, and of the personality of the taught – the pattern cannot be set through any of the current fashionable nostrums of wider participation of students, or of fledgling staff. It is meaningless to be asked either to defend the universities against the charges that they are undemocratic or to try to democratize them, because a university if it is to keep the correct emphasis upon its various functions must not be democratic, cannot indeed be democratic, but on the contrary should be and must be essentially and permanently hierarchic in structure.

Finally, the university that claims excellence must stand out against the current fashionable intellectual vice, the attempt to confuse the functions of institutions and of the roles of those who serve them. And this takes the particular form of demanding finally that everything be judged in the light of current political causes and controversies. The decline in religious belief and in the religious approach to life has meant that ministers of religion have increasingly sought to escape from their vocation by assuming the role of secular prophets in the vain hope that these incursions into the arena will recover for them their lost congregations. In the same way, men of science are told that to follow the path of investigation upon which their feet are set is insufficient, and that they must somehow assume responsibilities for the changes in society that science has helped to bring about, but in fields where they have no special competence to offer (on this point see the important lecture by Sir Ernst Chain, FRS (Chain 1970)). A scientist in the forum presents as incongruous a picture as a pop-star in a pulpit. It would be even worse if universities were to do here what some American universities have done, namely give corporate support to particular political attitudes which are not the special concern of universities and upon which men of goodwill may hold more than one opinion.

Universities will depart from the demands that the pursuit of excellence makes upon them if they envisage their social responsibilities as being more than two in number: to discover and teach the truth in so far as it lies in their power without respect to the popularity of particular truths, and this means withstanding demands made upon them with respect both to what is taught and to who teaches by the protagonists of particular ideologies; and to give to those briefly entrusted to their care before going out to play their respective roles in the wider world the maximum degree of care. They are, and still ought to be, pastoral in their approach to students.

My own belief is that some version of these views is widely held not only among a majority of university teachers but also among a majority of students. If we have seen a steady retreat from these principles on the part of the universities' representative figures, for instance on the part of the Committee of Vice-Chancellors and Principals in its constant policy of 'appeasement', and on the part of individual universities in their handling of their own internal pro-blems of organization and discipline, it is because so many teachers and students find it hard to realize the nature of the assault that is being made upon academic values, and understandably dislike the idea of giving up precious hours, weeks, months, and even years to fighting it off.

But there is another and perhaps more profound reason for our increasing acceptance of the unacceptable, and that lies in the fact that if what I have been saying is reactionary from the point of view of the universities themselves, it is even more so from the point of view of society as a whole. We live in a society whose values are increasingly collectivist and egalitarian; a university must by its nature be individualist and elitist. It must believe both in the absolute value of what it is trying to do, otherwise it would have no claims on society's resources to help it in its task, and in the inability of most individuals to partake in these activities – and of many even to appreciate their importance.

The egalitarian assault takes two very different forms. On the one hand, there are the arguments of crass materialism, or of philistinism in the sense that activities that cannot be measured in terms of a direct contribution to the national economic product are a waste of time and have no claim upon scarce resources. Thus, university education is equated with particular forms of vocational preparation and nothing else. And this materialism can take on a capitalist or a collectivist tinge. On the other hand, there is the assumption that one form of activity is as good as another, and one subject of study as good as another, and that the priorities hitherto accorded to the more important achievements of human thought, study, or artistic creativity are preserved only through class snobbery, and not for any intrinsic value they may possess. And this kind of pressure affects not merely the content of university curricula but also the preferred leisure activities of students, where the aim is not to sink individual identity in the common teenage culture, to the neglect of what were previously thought of as typically student leisure pursuits – formal debating, creative writing, the performance and study of classical music and drama, sports. By one of the innumerable paradoxes of the student movement, we find continuous demands that university staff and students should share all communal facilities – refectories, common-rooms and so on – just at a time when the interests and modes of behaviour of the young are so wilfully unsophisticated that they can hardly hope to find much in common with most of their elders.

Whether one takes the attitude to the problem of 'how many centres of excellence' implied in Professor Wolfe's paper or that in the above paragraphs, I think one comes to the same negative conclusion about the policy that has actually been followed in this country in the last couple of decades and is now being projected into the future, namely: the multiplication of institutions whether by upgrading or new foundation, all of which are supposedly of the same standard, and all of which are increasingly subjected to the grip of state-imposed norms. If the opponents of the 'binary system' get their way – and one could see this happening – the egalitarian impetus will have been further strengthened. Indeed, the fact that the Open University is giving degrees to those who begin with no formal preparation may actually render meaningless even the low standards demanded by some of the existing supposedly equal institutions. In other words we cannot cater for a mass demand for higher education without lowering the level of achievement at the top, unless we frankly accept the fact that just as men are unequal in themselves and in the demands that may be made upon them, so also are institutions.

If one argues this from the research side, the factors that have to be taken into account are physical plant and size of departments, and, perhaps most important of all for most subjects, libraries. Although the dimension of the library problem may be altered by the development of microfilm and microcard techniques, it will for some time be true, and perhaps always, that no truly great research-oriented university can exist a long way from a major library, and that the creation of such a library, unlike other physical plant, does not merely depend upon financial resources being available but is and must be the fruit of long development. Since it is my impression that libraries are the favourite targets for economy by the bureaucrats who rule us, the fight for adequate library expenditure, particularly for the great libraries, must be the first priority for anyone who believes that Britain ought to have at least some centres of excellence competitive on an international scale where the output of scientific and scholarly publication is the most obvious measuring-rod.

If one argues from my point of view, with the accent upon teaching and the life of the academic community, then of course the chance of centres of excellence being developed in a larger number of places would appear much greater. Here the limiting factors are personal, not material. I do not believe that there are at any one time more than a limited number of people suited to teach at the required intensity, or possessing the necessary set of attitudes. And some of those who are suited might require, to feel fully at ease with themselves and their pupils, some research opportunities either on or off the campus. Nor do I believe that there is a limitless number of students intellectually or temperamentally qualified for institutions of either kind of excellence.

All this need not mean that in a society changing as rapidly as ours is there is no need for opportunities of further education on an even wider scale than at present, both immediately following on school and later in life as technologies change. Nor should such further education necessarily be strictly vocational, though quite a high proportion of young people do find it important to know to what ends, in occupational and career terms, their education is being directed. But further education is not the same as higher education, and the present differentiation between the two made by educational administrators does not seem to me necessarily the right one. The argument about centres of excellence demands a reconsideration of the entire structure of postschool education with specific attention to the functions that different classes of institution do, or ideally should, perform.

In an age when respect for inherited social categories or individual achievement has been buried beneath an avalanche of status-seeking, and in which social and even intellectual relations are distorted by status-sensitivity, such a suggestion is bound to find little favour. But the alternatives seem to me to be grim indeed. If we cannot select then we can do nothing except to spread the butter so thin that we might as well be content with dry bread.

In recognizing the unpopularity of the elitist and anti-collectivist position which I have been sketching out, I find a curious paradox. The people who claim to be radical or progressive in fact deny the importance of the current university malaise, because they believe it can be cured within the present framework of organization and philosophy by mere changes in machinery, such as having more students on more committees and things of that kind. They seem to think that what we are witnessing is due largely to external causes: Vietnam, South Africa, the 'bomb', and so forth. Provided steam can be let off somehow, somewhere, things will somehow get put right again, and the pressures that are destroying university life and university standards will be neutralized. On the contrary I take the unrest very seriously indeed because I believe it to be inherent in what we have been trying to do, and that it will get worse rather than better if we follow the fashionable palliatives of our leaders. To say that student and faculty dissidence presents a problem of internal university organization only, is like saying that inflation, the symptom of a deep disease of civilization, is an economic problem.

To discuss the mechanics of getting centres of excellence or of preserving them – for we have some – before deciding whether our society wants them enough to pay for them, or is even prepared to tolerate them, seems to me, while very interesting as a technical exercise, all too likely just to remain one.

It has been suggested that I might wish to add a postscript about the project for the independent university. I do not wish to go into detail about something that is the product of much collective thinking. All I would want to say to connect it with my general argument is that were it not designed as a centre of excellence (at least in my sense), if not in its early stages in Professor Wolfe's, it would obviously have no appeal for me. What has interested me in the project is an attempt to test the hypothesis that some at least of our inadequacies in existing institutions derive from the increasing intervention of central government, and that this intervention is bound to go on increasing at an accelerating pace simply because the state is becoming almost the sole significant purveyor of funds. If this is true, then it follows that an institution whose constraints – and some financial constraints are inherent in any serious activity – were at least different ones, would perhaps permit some forms of experiment in both the organization of teaching and the recruitment of staff and students which are now impossible. Private endowments, real cost fees, student-loans, and all the other aspects of the project that its critics have seized upon are peripheral, not central, to it. They are means and not ends. What we want to see is whether it is possible at this juncture to create an institution in which there would be a greater degree of common ground between all its levels and a greater degree of common effort than we now find in many places. It is reactionary in that it relies upon certain values – competitiveness, selectivity, strenuousness, commitment, which are very unfashionable in places like Curzon Street. But since they are the values that made possible the great achievements of British universities in the past, and since the current values of laxity, undifferentiation, and egalitarianism seem to produce only frustration and disorder, I don't think the worse of the project for that.

REFERENCE

CHAIN, ERNST. 1970. *Social Responsibility and the Scientist in Modern Western Society*. London: Council of Christians and Jews.

Finance and control of universities: basic principles

W. H. F. BARNES

Of the many problems concerning the financing of universities I am concerned here with one only. Now that government finance through all channels forms 90 per cent of the recurrent and capital expenditure of British universities, how can they preserve the autonomy that is essential if they are to fulfil their proper role in the nation?

That universities should manage their own affairs is a truth that neither parliament nor the nation would have questioned twenty years ago. Yet in the last ten years much of this autonomy has been eroded and the threat to what remains increases yearly. How has this come about? What is this essential autonomy? How can it be preserved consistently with the very large sums now provided by the state to universities?

1 WHAT HAS HAPPENED?

In 1887 a government grant of £15,000 was made to the university colleges, that is, those institutions that were fledgling universities, financed like all other university institutions by endowments and public subscriptions. By 1906 there was a Continuing Committee under the Treasury to advise on the distribution of the grant. Then came the First World War. Wars not only impoverish, they breed state control and a liking for control. In 1919 a University Grants Committee (UGC) was set up under the Treasury to enquire into the universities' financial needs and to advise the government on the distribution of any grant. It was a characteristically British solution, preserving university autonomy in a masterly way by setting up as a buffer between universities and the government a predominantly academic body to advise on strictly financial matters. But there was even then a hint of what the future might reveal in a letter from Austen Chamberlain to the Chairman of the UGC about the impropriety of the government subsidizing activities 'unwarranted in the national interest' (Berdahl 1959). This phrase 'the national interest' and similar phrases were to recur frequently in years to come.

In 1926 the position of the universities, in relation to the grants made to them, was summed up by their spokesman, Sir Alfred Hopkinson: 'No one but ourselves can have any idea of how that money can best be spent from time to time. The doors are open and if we make fools of ourselves you can take it away. Inspect freely, but there must be absolutely no control.'

In more recent times there have been those who regard this attitude as unwarranted. In 1946, after the Second World War – which had left universities again in need of money for repair and expansion – Mrs Leah Manning asked the Treasury spokesman who was defending university autonomy in the House of Commons: 'Does he not think, as one of the largest contributors among those who pay the piper, he has some right to call the tune?' The Treasury spokesman did not think so.

Others were not so clear. In the same year the Barlow Committee on Manpower in Science and Technology saw no incompatibility between the universities' autonomy and 'the extension and improvement of the machinery for adjusting their policy to the needs of the country'. University autonomy now faced not the chill wind of intervention by the state or of strings attached to grants but the warmly mesmeric idea that, instead of simply educating people according to their ideals and standards, they were to have a 'policy' and that this policy was to form part of a great plan, excogitated presumably in Whitehall, to satisfy national needs, though of course the policy would need to be 'adjusted' to fit into this plan. These were the years in which the great illusion of a planned society was being incubated.

There was still a hope, however, that the innate good sense of ministers and parliament would continue to accept the idea of university autonomy. In 1957 Lord Attlee wrote: 'When I was in office, I steadily refused to try to increase the influence of the state on the universities. I know the objection heard that it is quite illogical to set up a body . . . give [it] money, and then do nothing to control it . . . There are matters in which I think it is better to have trust and I think this is one of them.'

In the last ten years the UGC system of preserving university autonomy has been eroded by a series of changes. The first, and perhaps the most important, was the breaking of the link between the UGC and the Treasury. Lord Murray of Newhaven, a former Chairman of the UGC, pointed out in 1955 that the UGC, being under the Treasury, had no fear that a department concerned with finance would question the Committee's advice on educational grounds and in this way 'exert an undue influence on university affairs'. The Treasury, as a matter of custom, accepted the UGC's recommendations on finance, and so did the Chancellor of the Exchequer. This was an essential element in a delicate equilibrium. The first crack in the system came when in 1962 the then Chancellor of the Exchequer for the first time cut the figure recommended. The Committee, though they may have considered resigning, did not in fact do so. As a result, the universities began to see the Committee as more closely aligned with government.

It soon became clear that the Treasury had no longer the will to sustain the relationship with the UGC and the universities. In the light of this fact the Committee on Higher Education, under Lord Robbins, recommended that a new ministry be set up to deal with the universities, the research council, and the arts. A minority of one recommended that the universities be placed under the Ministry of Education. After a brief interlude the universities in due course came under the Ministry of Education, a special arrangement being made for a separate permanent secretary. In 1965 this special arrangement was quietly dropped.

An indirect threat to university autonomy arose from the creation of the para-university system of giving degrees, through a council for national academic awards, to students in local authority colleges, an arrangement destined to blossom into the polytechnics and to give rise to the so-called 'binary' system of higher education. It has become a matter of faith with the Department of Education that the standards in these colleges are as high as in universities. These colleges do not have autonomy. If the premises are true, the conclusion is obvious.

In 1966 parliament conceded what it had in the interests of university autonomy consistently in the past refused, i.e. that the Comptroller and Auditor General should have access to the books and

162   W. H. F. BARNES

records of the UGC and the universities, a further diminution of university autonomy.

More significant in the long term were developments in the policy of the UGC. In the years of university expansion following the Robbins report and under a new chairman the Committee became more involved in giving 'guidance' to universities. From 1964 onwards it became a matter of negotiation between the UGC and each university what buildings should be erected out of the capital grants. In the letter setting out the recurrent grant for the quinquennium 1967–72 more general 'guidance' than ever before was included for all universities, and specific and explicit 'indications' were given to each university on the way its additional recurrent grant was to be spent. The net effect was to limit, so far as a large part of the additional grant was concerned, the university's freedom of choice.

How rapidly the ideal of university autonomy had faded became clear when, in 1968, the Prices and Incomes Board, reporting on academic salaries, produced recommendations that would, if accepted, have created a precedent for uninformed interference (of a kind from which the Treasury had scrupulously abstained) in matters at the heart of university affairs. Students' reports on lecturers were to be used to determine in part the latter's salaries. Teaching was to be encouraged in preference to research by a system of rewards. Merit awards for professors were to be made by a central body. Thanks to a number of individuals and organizations who protested promptly and decisively these recommendations were either immediately rejected by the government or in more leisurely fashion discussed out of existence.

2 UNIVERSITY AUTONOMY IN IDEA AND PRACTICE

I speak of 'university autonomy' rather than 'academic freedom' because it is a question of the institution's freedom to chart its own course, not of the freedom of its staff and students. No autonomy is absolute. It is not suggested by any responsible person that a university has the right to do what it likes with money it receives from any source. The government makes grants to universities for their essential functions, broadly identifiable though difficult to specify in detail. It has the right and duty to make sure that the grants are not used for other purposes. Hence the need for universities to be audited and to account for their expenditure. As far as the Comptroller and Auditor General has as his task to ensure that universities do not use their grants improperly, e.g. to finance subversion or entertain on an orgiastic scale, his activities are innocuous but perhaps also reduplicative since the university's auditors and published accounts already exercise this check.

More than the proper use of resources is involved. A university, while in essence an educational institution, is also a large-sized business. A medium-sized university of 5,000 students will have academic and ancillary staff of about another 2,000. It will put up buildings costing from one to two million pounds annually if it is expanding. It will have to acquire land, to furnish and maintain buildings, to pay salaries and wages to 2,000 people, to buy quantities of stocks and equipment. The procedures for doing all these things have a large common element with other businesses. They can be efficient or inefficient. The government has a right to be convinced that they are efficient. Efficiency in universities should be secured by advice and assistance rather than instruction; for the good reason that questions of efficiency merge imperceptibly into questions of aims and policies. A more efficient use of buildings by lengthening terms or by having a two-shift system raises a hornet's nest of academic issues about the aims and functions of the university. And when a body like the Prices and Incomes Board proposes that the efficiency of universities should be improved by their doing more teaching and less research, a fundamental policy issue has been pre-judged by a body totally unqualified to pronounce on such issues.

As well as being subject to audit and under a duty to make their administration efficient, there is an obligation to explain and defend policies and decisions. Universities must expect criticism and be ready to meet it as the price of their autonomy. If, as has happened more than once in their history, the universities in this country reach such a condition of inefficiency or disorder that they unmistakably fail to fulfil their proper function in the life of the nation, and prove incapable of the necessary effort to reform themselves, the state has not only a right but a duty to take action. In Britain the traditional course of action is a Royal Commission, the effect of which has never been to take away the autonomy of universities but to propose such reforms as may enable them to exercise their autonomy more effectively.

Within these general limitations, the autonomy of universities rests not on any idiosyncratic right to immunity from normal controls but on the fact that it is the best way to realize the values for which universities stand; the transmission of inherited knowledge, the free criticism of principles and ideas, the discovery of new truths, for all of which self-determination is an essential prerequisite. If the universities themselves have not the wisdom and expertise to control their own destiny, where is it to be found?

But it is not enough to talk in general terms. It is necessary, and possible, to list the areas of freedom that must at all costs be preserved and some of which are threatened. First, there is the formation of academic policy, involving the determination of subjects to be studied, curricula and methods, standards required for degrees, diplomas, etc., and the balance between teaching and research; second, the selection of staff and students; third, the allocation of resources between different purposes and the right to accept or reject offered grants or gifts; fourth, organization, administration, and internal discipline.

In some of these areas university autonomy has been under severe pressure for some time. There are fixed salary scales for non-professorial staff and an average salary for professors, as well as a ratio not to be exceeded of senior to junior academic staff. Finance allocated for academic salaries cannot be used for other purposes. The purpose of these controls is to achieve economy, and if they were to be removed some alternative method of realizing this end would be necessary.

It is over the allocation of resources to different purposes, particularly teaching and research, and the selection of subjects to be studied that control through the UGC has increased. In the past, earmarked grants have been made to develop particular subjects in particular universities. No one knows whether the university that accepted an earmarked grant would have received more, or less, in its block grant had there been no question of earmarking money for a particular purpose. More recently, earmarking has been replaced, or supplemented, by 'indications' of new developments. In spite of the diplomacy with which the UGC has handled this matter there is room for disquiet on the part of all who are not committed to the doctrine of national planning. For when all these 'indications' have been implemented a very considerable part of the additional resources provided to universities for their future development is pre-empted. The university's own policy-making is crippled.

The people of this country have recently expressed themselves as against a centrally planned society and in favour of individual initiative and responsibility. The government has spelled out beyond all possibility of misunderstanding that the tentacles of the state octopus are to relax their destructive grip on individuals and institutions. We may expect that the proposed Independent University will be encouraged in its effort to become the first self-supporting institution of its kind in Britain. Everyone should wish it well. But in no modern state can universities in general be freed from financial dependence. But it is your money and mine that supports universities. We are the pipers. It is for us to say who shall call the tune. I hope, and believe, that the principles of this government include the belief expressed by the late Sir Ernest Barker that 'while scope is demanded for the play of voluntary action, the demand is also made that the State should aid such action, and should aid it without impeding or seeking to contract its freedom'. In the present juncture what is needed is a restoration of the freedom that has been diminished. This can happen. It would be in line with the declared views of ministers; and civil servants, with their expert adaptability, may be expected to re-think the notions of 'national needs', 'overall manpower requirements', and 'settling priorities' in favour of ideas more in line with the principles of individual initiative and responsibility. Given the will, however, the means have still to be found.

3   FINANCE WITH FREEDOM

Once we get firmly out of our minds the confused notion, going back to the Barlow Committee's report, that somehow university autonomy can be reconciled with national planning, we can look at the problem in a new way. This requires us not to conflate but clearly to distinguish two separate relations in which the state stands to universities.

In the first place the universities have the function – not to be evaluated in economic terms – of continuing and spreading a tradition of learning and critical assessment of values throughout an increasing section of the community. To do this is analogous in a larger but more pervasive way to the task of galleries and museums, which preserve the heritage of art and spread its enjoyment and appreciation. In respect of this function the state is the patron of universities – a munificent patron of activities that penetrate a vast area of the community's life, but still a patron.

The temptation to convert patronage into control – not only, as it were, to finance the galleries but to choose the paintings – comes in the case of universities partly from the large sums of public money involved but more from the fact that universities, unlike galleries, are also necessary instruments for meeting certain economic needs. That is why students can, plausibly but mistakenly, say: 'We are not privileged people maintained at the nation's expense: we are an investment from which the nation expects to reap great dividends.' The mistake springs from the idea that the universities' primary function is to maximize the material welfare of the nation. The truth which underlies this mistake is that the state does need to use universities from time to time to meet specific requirements of this kind as they arise. As well as being a patron who seeks to encourage by its support, it is also at times a user who seeks to commission for its needs. At the moment these two functions are confused under the umbrella idea of planning for national needs which subtly influences the finance-cum-guidance policies of the UGC.

Now that national planning is dead and individuals are alive, the problem is to maximize the resources that the universities can properly be given 'without strings' to fulfil their primary educational function, while allowing also for specific grants in return for specific commitments. A small reform, which has often been suggested and has long been pressed for by the Vice-Chancellor's Committee, is that fees should be raised. This income comes through local authorities and is subject to no outside control. As a proportion of total university income it has sunk to 7 per cent. An increase from the present average fee per student of £70 to £250 would bring it up to 25 per cent. Such a change would certainly help the universities. But it is not enough.

I believe that consideration should be given, in the light of the state's two-fold role as patron of learning and user of university facilities, to moving away from the present system of *programme* financing to a new system of *formula* financing, with arrangements for *special purpose* financing when the government needs to use universities. Recurrent grants to universities would not be determined on the basis of what they proposed to teach or research. Instead they would be fixed by establishing a basic income unit – say, the annual cost of educating an undergraduate in the humanities.

The cost for an undergraduate in other subjects and for post-graduates would be fixed as a multiple of the basic income unit. The unit would have to be fixed to take account of all recurrent costs, including equipment, and after allowing for the research activities that are an essential part of university work. A major task of the UGC would be the fixing of this unit, together with the appropriate weighting for other subjects, in consultation with the universities and the government. The distribution of the global recurrent grant would be related directly to student intake and category. It would need to be reduced by the amount of income received through fees, if fees were retained as a feature of the system.

Formula finance would have some considerable advantages. It would give back to universities the freedom to determine the intake of students between different faculties; to lay emphasis on teaching or research; and, in general, to choose more freely between different categories of expenditure. There would be no temptation, for example, to spend money on equipment if it could be better spent in some other way, since money would not be earmarked for equipment as it is under the present system.

Such a change would present problems. Among these problems are: should academic salaries, like fees, be deducted from the sum to be fixed by formula, so that the uniform salary scales are maintained? If this were done, about one-third to a half of the recurrent grant would remain 'controlled'. If it were not done, the resulting competition between universities over salaries and teaching hours might be thought to have disadvantages that outweighed financial freedom. How would special-purpose finance operate? Should it be through the UGC or by direct negotiation with the Department of Education and perhaps other departments, as in the case of research grants from the government at the moment? For example, if the government decides more doctors are required, should the Department of Health, after negotiation with universities having medical faculties, provide the necessary finance? How should capital grants be made?

I make no claim to solving these problems. I plead only that the ideas be examined. Under our existing system we are drifting into a greater and greater state control of the universities which at no time has been specifically willed by parliament or any organ of government, and which no one has ever maintained as a principle or defended by argument. That formula finance is not impracticable is demonstrated by its existence in the university system of Ontario. What is needed is an examination of it at a high level in Britain as a remedy for the creeping erosion of university autonomy.

It is possible, though I hope it is not the case, that there are those in government who hold that, because public money supports, public authority must control. This is the principle of the French university system. It is a system no responsible and knowledgeable person would wish to see here. By contrast, the UGC system developed in Britain has been the object of admiration and imitation. It was described in the standard work *British Universities and the State* in 1959 as representing 'the most enlightened principles of State conduct towards universities'. This satisfaction, universally felt in 1959, has been dimmed but not extinguished by developments in the last decade.

There are reasons, outside the limits of my theme, for this change of attitude. The Robbins report assumed that, even though public expenditure on higher education would rise to unprecedented levels, the preservation and extension of autonomy in higher education needed no special defence though it required new mechanisms. The development of the binary system, by creating a non-autonomous sector of degree-giving higher education (against the Robbins recommendations) has given rise to demands for the abolition of the distinction between the two sectors. This has rebounded on the universities' claim to autonomy.

The universities themselves, regrettably, have provoked questioning in the public mind, which would have been unbelievable a decade ago, owing to the disruptive actions of a small minority of their students and staff and the difficulties these actions have created in resolving the issues involved. I believe these issues will be resolved. It would be a tragedy if the current unrest were, by its alienation of the public, to force greater state control upon the universities. It could happen. Already a Commons Select Committee, allotted the task of investigating student relations, found itself probing into all sorts of questions concerning university policy and government. I do not believe this kind of incidental investigation is satisfactory, either for parliament or for the universities. If the present disorder in universities was to increase intolerably – and it is only fair to point out that there *are* many peaceful and well-ordered universities – the proper remedy would be a Royal Commission.

The Robbins Committee did magnificent work in providing

information and statistics on every aspect of higher education and in surveying the whole of a very complex field studded with problems. It had the misfortune to be set up at least ten years too late. Some of its major recommendations, wise though they were, foundered upon intragovernment problems of responsibility, the onset of a steep decline in the nation's prosperity, and a worldwide upsurge of student unrest, as well as a too optimistic belief that the principle of university autonomy was an agreed and unchallengeable proposition. It is now a proposition that needs to be proclaimed, defended, and fought for in this nation which is its stronghold. The rector of Dijon University, analysing in 1965 the bureaucratic control by the state of universities in his country, concluded with the words: 'In taking away a university's autonomy and its independent existence, one takes away its life.' We are thankfully a long way from such a bureaucratic system. But it is better to treat a disease in its early stages rather than wait until it becomes fatal. That is why this problem of finance and control deserves our serious consideration.

REFERENCES

BERDAHL, ROBERT O. 1959. *British Universities and the State*. London.
COMMITTEE ON HIGHER EDUCATION. 1963. *Report* (Robbins report). Cmnd. 2154. London: HMSO.

Planning of higher education in the seventies

JOHN VAIZEY

The expansion of higher education has been a topic much discussed in many countries and not least in the United Kingdom. There have been a series of official reports and documents, of which the Robbins report was the largest and most significant, and a series of private studies from political groups and parties, from the Association of University Teachers and other professional groups, and from the students themselves. The latest document from official sources is Education Planning Paper (No. 2), 'Student numbers in higher education in England and Wales'. Scottish readers will perhaps forgive an Englishman if he concentrates on this document, even though a similar one has been issued for Scotland. The arguments presented for England and Wales on the one hand, and for Scotland on the other, are similar, and the conclusions to be drawn may be applied *mutatis mutandis* from one to the other.

The facts of past expansion are not in dispute. There has been throughout the world, both in developed countries and in developing countries, a vast increase in the number of students engaged in higher education.[1] This increase, in the developed countries at least, has been accompanied by no serious sign of a decline in academic quality, though in some countries where the provision of facilities has not kept pace with the increase in student numbers there is some evidence of a decline in teaching standards. Italy is an obvious case in point. This has not been the case in the United Kingdom. So far as could be seen in all parts of higher education, in the universities, the technical colleges, and polytechnics, or in the colleges of education, the increase in the number of students has not only been accompanied by an increase in their academic quality as measured by various indicators, but also by an improvement in the conditions under which students and teachers work.

The causes of the expansion are also clear. It has a great deal to do with the rise in *per capita* incomes throughout the developed world. It looks as though the income-elasticity of demand for higher education is exceptionally high. It is linked also to the spread of 'thirst' or 'hunger' for education, among members of the middle class, of whom a far higher proportion now seek academic preparation than before, and among the lower middle class and the more affluent artisans. There is as yet little evidence that this has affected the manual working class seriously. There is reason to suppose, too, that the development of higher education has been associated with increased demands for qualified manpower, particularly in the case of teachers and social workers, and of administrative and clerical officers of all grades. Demand for scientists and technologists is less fierce. At the same time entry to occupations tends to become increasingly formalized by a process of academic preparation in higher education institutions. Accountancy and the law are examples of this in Britain.

It is clear also that the future holds the possibility of a substantial expansion. If we look at the curve of the rate of growth of numbers of people with secondary education standardized for the size of the age-groups, it looks roughly as though decade by decade the rate of growth grows by 100 per cent, followed by $66\frac{2}{3}$ per cent, followed by $33\frac{1}{3}$ per cent. If this process is taking place in higher education, with a lag of a decade or so from secondary education, it looks as though we are probably still in the 100 per cent rate of increase per decade section of the curve. The probability is, therefore, that though the numbers will go on increasing, they will go on increasing as they have been in secondary education, but soon at a diminishing rate.[2] The absolute numbers, of course, will continue to increase substantially. The reasons behind this projected increase are of the same order as those that have been adumbrated for the previous expansion, and there is no serious reason to suppose that any of the motivations that have affected the families whose children seek higher education have weakened. It may well be, of course, that over relatively short periods social barriers or economic difficulties may well affect the smoothness of the curve, but about its tendency in the long run there is little dispute. As an example, the number of entrants to fulltime higher education in 1962 was 60,000; the number in 1967 was 107,000. In 1976, according to the Department of Education and Science's paper, it will be of the order of 170,000, and the 1981 figures may be 218,000. These figures represent a substantial increase over the figures projected in Robbins. This is not a serious matter, as the Robbins projection was almost certainly deliberately pitched too low, since the higher projections of Robbins were more likely to frighten than to persuade the Treasury and conservative public opinion and were therefore not published. There are reasons to suppose that even the present projections are too low, since they depend upon a line drawn between an arithmetic growth-curve of secondary leavers and a geometric growth-curve, and it appears as though no adequate anticipation is being made of the effects of the raising of the school-leaving age or of the effects of secondary reorganization. This is unlikely to affect the number of entrants much in the short run, but to have a profound effect in the longer run. The number of students, therefore, is likely to increase more than is now supposed.

I was once severely taken to task by a reviewer for basing projections of future numbers in higher education in my contribution to Professor Wilfred Beckerman's book, *The British Economy in 1975*, on foreign experience. In fact this was not so. I made a perfectly orthodox projection on the basis of likely economic and social relationships, but I drew attention in one paragraph, at the editor's suggestion, to the fact that this projected expansion was by no means unusual, and indeed fell on the relatively low side in comparison with our European neighbours. The reviewer quite rightly pointed out that something that I did not assert was not correct, namely, that the fact that foreigners did it did not mean that we had to do it too. Nevertheless, it is of course interesting that most countries, and particularly countries whose economy and society is roughly similar to our own, have been through the same experience. And it still remains the case that the United Kingdom expansion in student numbers is relatively lower than our neighbours', though it is also fair to say that the number of graduates is higher and remains so. This is because wastage rates here are lower than elsewhere.

The rate of growth in student numbers is therefore likely in the future to diminish, but the absolute size of the student population will of course increase. We are obviously within sight of having to make arrangements for a million or more students in the United Kingdom.

It is true that quite unprecedented social changes may occur which would completely transform this situation, but happily cataclysmic social change is rare and in any case is unlikely to lead to a sudden diminution in the desire for higher and further education. I will leave to others the discussion of its social consequences and of the academic nature of the provision that should be made. I believe that the social consequences in one sense are likely to be profound, mainly because England in particular has never before had a large class of students in the way that American and continental society has become accustomed to. In another sense, I believe the effect will be less profound, since the evidence convinces me at least that the increase in the number of higher education places is not itself a major element in increasing the rate of social mobility, but rather reflects social mobility in our society which seems little different now from what it has been in the past. With regard to the academic consequences, too, clearly, there is likely to be and has already been a substantial change in the nature of the courses that are offered. So far, one must insist that there is no evidence of any decline in academic quality, and considerable evidence of a rise, more especially in the relatively underprivileged sectors of the colleges of education and of further education. But it is manifestly clear that the nature of the curriculum, and in particular the techniques of teaching, are likely to go through a major process of change in the coming decades. That this is affected by profound cultural shifts cannot be doubted, and in particular it is obviously affected by the relative change in the social position of different age-groups, and by such matters as the lowering of the age of majority.

It is on the economic consequences, however, that I wish to dwell. I will use, if I may, two works for my text. The first is the Education Planning Paper already referred to, the others are the reports of the Gulbenkian Foundation study which has been conducted, under my direction, into the economics of education (Vaizey *et al.* 1968–71). The Education Planning Paper is in many ways an astonishing document, since it is both pedestrian and ill informed. It adumbrates in its first section a series of views of the future of higher education that are jejune in the extreme. It distinguishes between the so-called manpower approach, that is to say the demand for higher education that can be calculated from the likely change in the requirements of the economy for those who possess some occupational qualification;

the social-demand approach, that is to say what has commonly come to be known as the rise in the demand for higher education arising from causes that are largely explained by the process of social change and the rise in that part of the national income going to consumption; and the so-called rate-of-return approach. The rate-of-return approach has been described often. It is an attempt to relate the costs of education to the expected changes in people's earnings which they receive as a consequence of their education. The summaries of these issues, as presented in the paper, can mean little to those who have not already heard of them, and must be regarded as seriously inadequate by those who have devoted any attention at all in the past to considering them. Nowhere do they meet the serious problems that have been presented by critics of all three points of view. This is especially true of the so-called rate-of-return approach. The rate-of-return approach may be criticized under three headings. First, that the notion of capital that is used is a highly tendentious and very simple one which is not acceptable to the majority of English economists who have written on the nature of capital; second, that there are grave doubts about using cross-section income data for a long time-series such as an expected working life; and third, that there are even graver doubts about the causal relationship between education and subsequent income. There is a paradox to which Mr Clark Kerr of the University of California has often referred, that whereas the evidence from sociology and psychology tends to show little relationship between education and subsequent social mobility, the rate-of-return analysis is posited upon the assumption that people's social position can go up and down like yo-yos on a string. The whole analysis of all these three approaches in this document rests furthermore upon a type of marginal economic analysis that is quite unacceptable to many economists. There can be no objection to people holding marginalist views if they wish to do so. Considerable exception may be taken, however, to anonymous official publications putting these views forward as though they represent the considered views of Whitehall. As a matter of fact, the senior economic advisers, both to the present and to the past administration, were not marginal economists. Indeed, one of them, Lord Roberthall wrote one of the fundamental articles attacking marginalism in pricing policy before the war (see Hall and Hitch 1966). There is no reason to suppose, many of us think, that there is a connection between wages on the one hand and the process of wage-determination that are adumbrated in perfect competition theory on the other. This is an important point, and one of profound philosophical import since it affects the whole nature of the way in which you look at society. I shall revert to this theme later.

The conclusion that I would draw from my own work over the years on this and other topics is that the demand for education, which has been increasing so rapidly, is one of those major cultural and social changes that periodically overtake societies. It may be compared to the Puritan revolution in the late sixteenth and seventeenth centuries, or the rise of Methodism, or to the change in the social position of women which occurred in the early twentieth century, and to the change in the self-consciousness of the black races which is occurring now. That is to say, it is a change in the view that families and young people take of how they should lead their lives up to the age of twenty-two or twenty-three, and it is a change in the nature of the way that they look at life itself. This has had and will have economic consequences in the sense that a general rise in the number of those who take an educated and rationalist view of life will automatically affect both patterns of consumption and attitudes to work. There is no doubt also that there is a requirement in the economy for specific kinds of skills that can only be acquired through the education and training process. I may add, parenthetically, that I believe the evidence suggests that those who wish to receive a specific training in a skill can often acquire it very much more rapidly than educators and trainers believe. I am perennially surprised when I visit the developing countries by the number of completely uneducated people who have picked up what appear to me to be fairly complex skills. This reinforces my view that most education and training represents almost a social-anthropological process of induction rather than a necessary relationship between the process of acquiring a skill and the subsequent exercise of that skill. However, I do not wish to be pedantic in this matter, and I prefer to assume for the sake of argument that some at least of those who are educated and trained in higher education are educated and trained because they are likely to require this education and training in their occupations.

My own view is that as productivity in the economy increases, this is largely due to the incorporation of technological innovation into the capital structure of the economy and the skills embodied in the labour force adapt to this changing capital structure. I also think that only a comparatively small part of the amount of technological and scientific advance is actually incorporated in the economy, and a great deal of what is incorporated is borrowed from abroad through the process of the international flow of capital and the international flow of ideas. The greater part of our British scientific effort and some of our technological effort is likely to have had little or no relevance to our economic development. I would not think it could be seriously argued, therefore, that the reason for the growth in higher education was strictly economic. Indeed, I prefer to turn the argument on its head and argue that the reason why we have economic growth is because among other things the people need education. I think this poses a radical cultural question, and, in particular, what kind of education they need. I think, too, that if the education is not to be in any simple-minded way immediately useful then it is possible for it to be culturally far more adventurous, and in particular we could diminish the sense of urgency with which people seek to acquire qualifications, at least in the greater part of the education system. I would also argue, and this will form a substantial part of the later part of my paper, that substantial numbers of people who are now being directed by one means or other into avenues that lead into science and technology need not be so directed if they do not want to be, and that we need not reproach ourselves if this sector of our education system does not continue to be as significant numerically in the future as it has been in the past. Indeed, I would go so far as to say that the major part of science education ought to be undertaken because we believe in the value of science in our culture, and that we only 'need' scientists in the same sort of way as we 'need' historians, that is to say, because the culture is more vigorous and rich if people have studied science and enjoy doing it.

The economic and financial costs of the expansion are highly relevant to the main theme of this conference, which I take to be the likely changes in the structure, content, style, and control of higher education. The first point to be made is that, whichever way one looks at it, if the number of students goes up over the next ten to fifteen years by two to three times the present number, it is certainly true that both the real economic burden and the financial costs will substantially increase. A *caveat* perhaps should be entered at this stage, that the calculation of all these costs and of the financial burden depends upon many assumptions, and the purpose of any academic discussion of these matters is to make as many assumptions as possible explicit. One that has been implicit in all the discussions so far is the continuation of full employment. If there is no continuation of full employment, then the expansion of higher education will not only not use up real resources in any meaningful sense, but it may also play an important part in counter-deflationary mechanisms of increasing public expenditure. This may seem improbable at present, but economic circumstances do change and change suddenly. It is worth pointing out that one of the assumptions underlying much recent work is of a continuation of the present. Indeed, the other assumption is one of continuous economic growth, but only in the exceptionally unlikely circumstances that the British economic growth-rate doubles would the proportion of the national income devoted to higher education remain constant. Personally, I find this nothing serious to worry about, both because the composition of the national income changes through time and has included a diminishing proportion of the national income spent on food, and an increasing proportion spent on transport, entertainment, leisure, and education; and also because purely at the level of public finance it is extremely improbable that a major social service with considerable pressure to expand could over the years be inhibited by political decisions to keep the level of expenditure at present levels. It is quite unrealistic to assume that any cabinet, whether labour or conservative, could stand idly by while the number of A levels required for admission to the universities rose from two to three to four to five, and it is this which is implicit in any notion that things could be kept as they are. That the resources will be found, and the finance will be found to support the resources seems to me to be a matter beyond question. What is not beyond question, however, is the actual amount of resources likely to be required and the methods that will be adopted to pay for them.

If I may, I will base this part of the discussion once more on projections which are made in the *Education Planning Paper*, 2. The first point concerns the so-called income forgone. This is what the students might have earned had they not been students. This seems an exceptionally metaphysical (in the pejorative sense) concept. The difficulty is that this notion is not included in conventional national-income accounting. National-income accounting does include magnitudes of notional payments that are not actually understood the purposes for which it will be used, and has not fully understood the concepts that it is using, the document is even more unhelpful since it omits maintenance costs paid through the form of student grants. These student grants are likely to be a matter of considerable public discussion and of considerable significance in the political economy of education over the coming years.

Turning now to the notional unit costs of higher education, two series of calculations are made, both of which are seriously misleading. The first assumes that the subject-balance in the universities, colleges of education, and further education will remain what it now is. And this is implausible.

This is the place for a disquisition on the place of science and technology in higher education in the next ten to twenty years. It has already been argued that there is only a very loose connection between expenditure on science and technology research and economic development. The incorporation of scientific research into technological progress and of technological progress into new capital equipment is slow and dodgy. That it occurs there is no doubt. That it is connected to substantial increases in the amount of expenditure on scientific research has never been shown. And, incidentally, the techniques suggested in a recent DES publication on this matter (1969) suggest that marginalist analysis is not much help here. Professor Kaldor and others have proposed models that are particularly suggestive in this area. The implication that I draw from their models is that science and technology as such are not particularly important for economic growth (this leaves on one side altogether the question of the social importance in any absolute sense of economic growth itself).

Second, there is little evidence that the country in any meaningful sense 'needs' to increase the supply of engineers and scientists at the rate at which policy has been increasing the number of places. Some economists have argued that the students themselves realize this, that the likely earnings of scientists and engineers are considerably lower than those in other fields, and for this reason people do not take up scientific and technological places in the same numbers that they do places in the arts and social sciences. Other arguments have been advanced, that the science and technology courses are excessively dull and unattractive, that the teaching in science and technology is bad, that students under the influence of drugs and modern pop culture are unwilling to undertake difficult and hard

made, for example, imputed house rents for owner-occupied ho
but national-income calculation has always been conserv
about this, because in principle there is no limit to the numb
costs and benefits that could be added to the national in
accounts as we have them. The benefits, for example, of na
parks and the rural beauty of England, the unpleasantness of a
noise, and so on, could all be added to and subtracted fro
Gross National Product figures.[3] The fact that this is not
diminishes the validity of the national-income accounts as ind
of economic, social, and political welfare, as has been familia
the national income accounts were first theoretically devi
Bowley and Pigou. The difficulty, however, arises when one
lar adjustment is made, namely the inclusion of notional
forgone, and is compared with the national-income account
lated on what has become a conventional basis. If there is
departure in one direction, there must be a departure in ot
must then also include, for example, in the positive sid
national-income account the sheer pleasure that students
being students, and not having to work for a living in dr
I believe myself that this is becoming increasingly importar
and more young people take an existentialist view of the
of the happiness of the moment. There is a further techn
ment against the inclusion of income forgone in the costs
education as suggested in the *Education Planning Paper*
that the incomes taken for comparison are almost certai
high. While it is true of a few thousand students out of
or so students at present in fulltime higher education, if
employment, that they might earn much the same rate
those going to their contemporaries, it is wholly imi
assume that a doubling in the number of students will n
whole structure of the labour market. We have no id
incomes they are forgoing would be. It is also quite inval
the costs of income forgone as a deduction from the nat
without making allowances for subsequent increases in
income which conceivably *might* occur, though in my
would not occur in any substantial amount, from th
work of the students. It is therefore surprising to see th
in the *Education Planning Paper* including income fo
important, as the calculations include a substantia
income forgone. Because the author of the documer

subjects and therefore take up things like economics and sociology. About the genesis of the students' distaste for science and technology I am agnostic, but about its existence there can be no dispute. I am one of those who finds no national reason why the number of scientists and technologists should be increased. I think it is important to maintain scientific and technological education, both because there is a minimum number of scientists and technologists needed to keep the economy going (and the education system teaching science and technology, I may add), and also because science and technology are obviously an important part of culture. Nobody, I think, is proposing that science and technology as such should die out in a way that some other disciplines have almost done. But the issue is whether or not they should be given quite the same level of provision in the increments of additional higher education as they have been over the last fifteen years. Here the experience of the open-ended entry to further education is particularly interesting. The polytechnics, which are singularly misnamed and ought to be called 'polyartnics', are of course expanding rapidly in the fields of social sciences and the humanities, and there is no doubt that this is where the student demand is. Since I take the view that the growth of science and technology as such has no high national priority, my own view would be that there is no great danger in acceding to what the students want, which is more places in the humanities and in the social sciences. I would hope that there would be more bridging courses; I would hope that the English and Welsh would adopt the sensible Scots system of not allowing early specialization at school; and I would hope that the universities and other institutions of higher learning would play their part in allowing students, by means of a credit system or whatever, to combine things that at the moment are not often combined. But that this would lead to a *lower* increase in the provision of places in the sciences, and more especially in the very expensive sciences and technologies, I have no doubt whatever. In particular, I would suspect that physics and chemistry are now fully provided for, for at least the decade of the seventies. Such expansion as there is likely to be would probably be in biology. Now the significance of this is, of course, that the reason why university unit costs are higher than those of other sectors of higher education is partly because the universities contain so high a proportion of science and technology places. The attack that has been mounted over the years against the universities, that they are out-dated, out-moded, anti-scientific, and so on, has I think always been absurd, but nowhere has it been more particularly absurd than in the field of science. Oxford, the university usually held up for ridicule, has over a hundred Fellows of the Royal Society and five Nobel Prize-winners on its faculty. I think there is no technological university or polytechnic proud of its scientific and engineering effort that could begin to rival this number.

If the predilection for science and technology were abandoned and places were provided only on student demand, the unit cost of additional places in the universities would drop dramatically. Second, of course, there is a significant difference between the cost per student year and the cost per completed graduate. This is affected, of course by wastage and drop-out rates. Wastage and drop-out rates in the sciences and technologies are significantly higher than in the arts and humanities. It follows therefore that the cost of an arts or humanities graduate is very significantly lower than the cost of a science graduate, not only because the cost per student year is less, but because there are fewer student years per graduate.

These two considerations completely alter the relative structure of unit costs per graduate of each sector. For planning purposes, clearly, this is a highly relevant consideration. The universities have been regarded as a high-cost sector; the planning exercise is based on the assumption that they will continue to be so. It seems that they need not be so – quite apart from such considerations of the likely fall in unit costs as economies of scale are reaped. (To this must be added the ultimate absurdity of the Planning Document. The income forgone is higher for undergraduates in universities (£755 p.a.), than for students in further education (£690). If a policy were adopted to increase the university entry and diminish the entry to further education the income forgone would rise – for exactly the same people!)

The view that must be taken ultimately, then, is that the Planning Document is not only poor in quality but is systematically biased against the universities. It needs to be replaced by a series of projections on different assumptions, and any reasonable series of assumptions is likely to reduce the total costs of expansion, and to change the relative costs of different sectors. This is a not unimportant conclusion.

NOTES

[1] See OECD Conference on *Policies for Educational Growth*, Vol. II. Paris: 1971.

[2] Standardizing for the size of age-cohorts.

[3] In view of comments by a philosopher at the seminar, it should be noted that this argument, while formally impeccable, is in the nature of a *reductio ad absurdum*. The absurd, of course, is Planning Paper 2.

REFERENCES

BECKERMAN, WILFRED. 1966. *The British Economy in 1975*. Cambridge: Cambridge University Press.

HALL, R. and HITCH, C. J. 1966. In T. Wilson and P. W. S. Andrews (eds), *Oxford Studies in the Price Mechanism*. London: Oxford University Press.

DEPARTMENT OF EDUCATION AND SCIENCE. 1969. *An Attempt to Quantify the Economic Benefits of Scientific Research*. Science Policy Studies No. 4. London: HMSO.

VAIZEY, JOHN, *et al*. 1968–71. *The Economics of Educational Costing*. Five volumes. Lisbon: Centro de Economia e Financas.

Subject Index

academic quality, 171–2, 174
alienation, 3, 168
America, *see* USA
aristocracy, 1–2, 8, 11
arts specialist(s), 65, 66, 67, 68, 69

Barlow Committee on Manpower in Science and Technology, 160, 165
binary system, of higher education, 29, 39, 43, 80, 84, 98, 103, 115–28, 132, 155, 161, 168
biologist(s), 66, 67, 69, 70
Britain, *see* UK
Brockenhurst Comprehensive College, 93–4
Bulgaria, 32

California Institute of Oriental Studies, 34
Caltech, 34
Canada, 56
central institutions, ix, 101, 128
Church, 2–3, 19
  of England, 7, 21
civil service, 7, 8, 10
college(s), 15
  community, 99, 100, 130, 131, 133
  comprehensive, 92–5, 99
  of education, 75, 100–14, 119, 127, 171, 180
  of further education, 20, 75, 96, 108, 110, 180
  junior, 34, 37, 85–100
  sixth-form, 75, 91
  state, 87, 88, 89
  technical, 94, 96, 171
  of technology, 75, 118, 132
  tertiary, 83–4
commerce, 9, 11, 117, 118, 119, 123

convergers, 51, 66–7, 68, 69, 70
cost of education, *see* finance
Council for National Academic Awards, 15, 26, 119, 120–1, 161
courses
  block-release, 121
  day-release, 121
  parttime, 41, 42, 96, 118
  sandwich, 119, 121
creative writer(s), 67, 69
credits, accumulation of, 124, 126, 181
Czechoslovakia, 33

degree(s), 83, 116
  external, 26, 120
  general, 22, 26
  higher, 39
  honours, 22, 51, 53
  PhD, 25, 36, 39, 142
  right to grant, 15, 16, 45, 87, 116, 120
  see also credits
dissenting academies, 5, 15
divergers, 66–7, 68, 69, 70
drop-out rate, 30, 31, 33, 41–3, 44, 82, 182
  see also wastage

Eastern Europe, 32, 33
education
  further, 75, 115, 127, 156, 175
  general, 80, 82
  parttime, 115, 121–4, 125
  postgraduate, 139–50
  primary, 31, 38, 83, 112
  secondary, 18, 31, 38, 40, 41, 76, 80, 83, 102, 112, 172
  structure of, 29–46, 75, 95

education—*contd.*
    tertiary, 18, 35, 38, 40, 75, 81
        102, 115, 117, 127, 128
    for women, 122–3
    see also higher education
Education Act (1944), 11
Education Planning Paper (No. 2),
    171, 174, 178, 179
Educational Institute of Scotland, 15
elite, 11
    academic, 20, 34
    administrative, 30
    ecclesiastical, 3
    governing, 7, 9, 11
    intellectual, 25
    scientific, 30
    social, 2, 34
elitism, 56, 127, 157
    undergraduate, 24–5
    university, ix, 18, 23, 26, 115, 154
engineer(s), 64, 65, 180
engineering, 23, 30, 40, 55–61, 117
    and science, 57
    see also technology
England, 1–12, 17, 18, 22, 23, 24, 32,
    47, 70, 76, 79, 81, 83, 91–5, 97, 102–5,
    109, 111, 112, 127, 133, 171, 174, 181
excellence
    academic, x, 151
    centres of, ix, 26, 90, 132, 151–8
expansion
    economic consequences of, 174–82
    of higher education, 48, 49, 57, 79,
        87, 129–30, 131, 171–83
    manpower approach to, 174
    rate-of-return approach to, 175
    social-demand approach to, 175
    of universities, 1, 47, 48–50, 171

finance (cost)
    of higher education, 79, 80, 98,
        115, 116, 123, 127, 135, 177–
        182
    of universities, 20, 25, 127, 157,
        159–69, 181
First World War, 2, 11, 159
Fleming Committee, 29
Foothill College, 89
France, 11, 30, 32, 39, 55, 129, 168
freedom, academic, 33, 162, 164

General Certificate of Education, 76–7,
    83, 94, 115

Germany
    East, 31, 32
    West, x, 6, 18, 20, 25, 29, 30, 32,
        33, 34, 41, 43, 56, 131–2, 133,
        136
government (state)
    and education, 99
    as patron, 26–7, 165–6
    and universities, 21–2, 25, 26, 27,
        29, 33, 36, 38, 59, 117, 157, 159–
        169
grandes écoles (France), 30
grants
    research, 24, 36
    student, 24–5, 180

Herzen Institute, Leningrad, 40
higher education, ix, x, 1, 6, 10, 13,
    22, 25, 26, 57, 60, 75, 76, 83, 87, 112,
    115–27, 139–50, 156
    expansion of, 48, 49, 57, 79, 87
        129–30, 131, 171–83
    finance (cost) of, 79, 80, 98, 115,
        116, 123, 127, 135, 177–82
    structure of, 29–46, 80, 82, 108
    types of, 129–37
    see also binary system; colleges;
        education; polytechnics; uni-
        versities
Hochschulen (Germany), 10, 34, 38

Indian Empire, 7, 10, 11
Industrial Revolution, 1, 5
Industrial Training Act, 76
industry, ix, 56, 88, 117, 118, 119, 121,
    123, 132, 141
innovation, educational, 47, 50–4, 72,
    99, 112
Inns of Court, 2, 3
Ireland, 6, 10, 17, 18, 19, 27, 47, 70
Italy, 171

James Committee, ix
junior college(s), 34, 37, 85–100
    in California, 86–91, 96, 98
    in Hampshire, 91–5, 99
    objectives of, 90
    relations with university, 98
    in Scotland, 95–8

Kalinin Polytechnic, Leningrad, 40

latency period, 68, 71
Lenin Institute, Moscow, 40

liberal arts, 84, 130, 134
   colleges, 34, 107, 110
libraries, 117, 155–6
London School of Economics, 13

Manchester Institute of Science and
   Technology, 146, 147
Markov chain, 148–50
Massachusetts Institute of Technology, 35
mathematician(s), 65, 67
   see also subjects
Max-Planck-Gesellschaft, 32
medical specialists, 65, 70–1
   see also subjects
Mennonite Biblical Seminary, 34

Open University, the, 26, 47, 118,
   124–6, 155
Owens College, Manchester, 5

parttime
   courses, 41, 42, 96, 118
   education, 115, 121–4, 125
   students, 10, 41, 119, 126
patronage, by the state, 26–7, 165–6
philosopher(s), 69–70
   see also subjects
physicist(s), 65, 67, 69
polytechnics, 26, 59, 101, 108, 110,
   118–19, 127, 132, 134, 141, 146, 161,
   171, 181, 182
postgraduate
   education, 139–50
   students, 39, 139–50
professional
   commitment, 107, 113
   image (stereotype), 65, 67, 68
   training, 9, 10, 29, 30, 38, 40, 43, 58
   see also vocational training
psychologist(s), 63, 65, 68, 69
Puritan movement, 2, 5, 176

reality testing, 68
research, 17, 20, 25, 32, 39, 87, 90, 119,
   131, 133, 139, 141, 142, 143, 146,
   151, 155, 156, 162, 167, 180
   educational, 63–4
   grants, 24, 36
Riga Polytechnic, Moscow, 40
Robbins Committee Report, 13, 103,
   108, 111, 116, 120, 127, 161, 162,
   168, 171, 173

Rumania, 31, 32
Russia, *see* USSR

Scandinavia, 32
Science Research Council, 135
scientist(s), 9, 65, 66, 67, 68, 69
   see also subjects
school, 15, 78–9
   comprehensive, 86, 92, 93, 96, 131
   secondary, x, 17, 20, 81
   and university, ix, 17, 27
Scotland, ix, x, 6, 10, 14, 16, 17, 18, 19,
   20, 21, 22, 23, 24, 25, 26, 33, 44, 47,
   70, 76, 77, 79, 81, 83, 95–8, 101, 102–5,
   110–11, 112, 113, 127, 128, 133, 134,
   171, 181
Scottish Certificate of Education, 77,
   97
Second World War, 11, 160
selection, 31–2, 42, 56, 77, 82, 84, 94,
   96, 117, 129, 131, 132, 135
social scientist(s), 63, 67, 69, 70
   see also subjects
specialization, 38, 53, 66, 76, 77, 80,
   82, 122, 134, 141, 181
student(s), 155, 162, 166, 179, 180–1
   grants, 24–5, 180
   numbers of, 10, 18, 19, 34–5, 41,
      127, 171
   overseas, 140, 143, 147
   parttime, 10, 41, 119, 126
   postgraduate, 39, 139–50
   rise in numbers, 4, 48, 49, 79, 80,
      115
   and university government, 52,
      104
   unrest, 50, 130, 157, 168
subjects
   balance of, 1, 2, 4, 9, 57, 64, 180
   classics, 6, 9, 21
   engineering, 23, 117
   history, 4, 6, 9, 53
   languages, 23, 53
   law, 6, 9, 29, 30, 117
   logic, 2–3, 53
   mathematics, 21, 53
   medicine, 6, 9, 18, 22, 23, 29, 30,
      117
   natural science, 6, 9
   philosophy, 4, 6, 9
   psychological basis of choice, 63–
      73
   rhetoric, 4

subjects—*contd.*
science, 57, 177, 180–2
social science, 181
technology, 177, 180–2

teaching, 30, 77, 90, 119, 133
methods, 125
training for, ix, 18, 22, 23, 40, 42, 101–14, 118, 132
university, 14, 17, 32, 36, 72, 131, 151, 162
technology, 177, 180–2
tekhnikumy (USSR), 40
Totton Comprehensive College, 93

UK, x, 13, 14, 16, 25, 29, 31, 32, 39, 43, 55, 56, 57, 76, 81, 82, 85, 86, 87, 89, 116, 119, 129, 132, 139–47, 156, 159–169, 171, 173, 178
USA, x, 8, 15, 20, 25, 34–7, 42, 56, 57, 65, 76, 83, 85, 86–91, 97, 98, 111, 120, 121, 124, 129, 130–1, 132, 133, 135, 136, 141, 152, 153, 174, 175
USSR, 29, 37–42, 44, 56, 121, 129, 141
unions, teachers, ix
Association of Teachers in Colleges and Departments of Education, 105, 107, 108, 109, 110
university(s)
autonomy of, 49, 159–69
as a business, 163
categorization of, 13–15
as centres of excellence, 151–8
as centres of innovation, 47, 50–4, 72
comprehensive, 131
drop-out rate, 30, 31, 33, 41–2, 44, 82, 182
entrance (requirements), 13, 18, 83, 109
in Europe, 30–3, 134
as examination board, 14
expansion of, 1, 47, 48–50, 171
finance of, 20, 25, 127, 157, 159–169, 181
and government (state), 21–2, 25, 26, 27, 29, 33, 36, 38, 59, 117, 157, 159–69
history of, 1–12
independent, 157–8, 165
management of, 48, 49, 51–2
and other higher education, ix, 29, 82, 86, 98, 106–7, 119

private foundation, 46–7
role (function) of, ix, x, 1, 9, 10, 11, 13, 15, 16, 38, 42, 47–54, 110, 117, 132–4
and school, ix, 17, 27
and teacher training, 101, 103, 106–8, 110, 112
teaching, 14, 17, 32, 36, 72, 131, 151, 162
in USA, 34–7
in USSR, 37–42
University
Aberdeen, 23, 27, 104
Aberystwyth, 13
Andersonian, 15
Berkeley, 34, 35
Bielefeld, 33
Birmingham, 103, 143, 144, 145, 146, 147
Bochum, 33
Bristol, 103, 110, 143, 144, 145, 147
California, 34, 36, 37, 175
Cambridge, x, 3, 5, 6, 7, 9, 10, 11, 13, 14, 16, 17, 18, 19, 21, 22, 23, 24, 25, 117, 142, 143, 144, 145, 146, 147
Chicago, 34
Cologne, 30
Columbia, 35, 36
Cornell, 56
Corpus Christi, Texas, 35
Dublin, 13, 14
Dundee, 104, 110, 111
Durham, 13, 14, 16, 21, 23, 25, 143, 144
East Anglia, 47, 49, 50
Edinburgh, ix, 13, 16, 17, 18, 22, 35, 58, 90, 104, 143, 144, 145, 146, 147
Essex, 47, 49, 50
Freiburg, 30
Georgia, 36
Glasgow, 16, 19, 22, 104, 143, 144, 145, 146
Grenoble, 30
Harvard, 36
Heidelberg, 30
Heriot-Watt, 110
Hull, 13
Keele, 47, 49, 51, 52, 53, 105
Kent, 47
Kent State, 35, 37

Konstanz, 33
Lancaster, 47, 49, 53, 116
Leeds, 143, 144, 145, 146, 147
Leningrad, 40
Liverpool, 143, 144, 145, 146, 147
London, 5, 6, 13, 14, 15, 16, 17, 18, 19, 21, 23, 25, 119, 142, 143, 144, 145, 146, 147
Lyons, 30
Manchester, 13, 14, 19, 21, 25, 143, 144, 145, 146, 147
Michigan, 36
Missouri, 37
Moscow, 40
New York State, 34, 37, 111
North Carolina, 36, 37
Nottingham, 143, 144, 145, 146, 147
Ohio State, 34
the Open, 26, 47, 118, 124–6, 155
Oxford, x, 3, 4, 5, 6, 7, 8, 9, 10, 11, 13, 14, 15, 16, 17, 18, 19, 21, 22, 23, 24, 25, 70, 117, 134, 142, 143, 144, 145, 146, 147, 182
Penn State, 34, 36
Princeton, 35, 36
Reading, 147
St Andrews, 13, 22, 23, 134, 135
Sheffield, 146, 147
Southampton, 147
Sorbonne, 30

Stanford, 56
Stirling, 47, 48, 49, 50, 52, 53, 105, 110
Strathclyde, 110
Sussex, 47, 49, 52, 53, 116
Ulster, 47
Vassar, 35
Virginia, 6, 25
Warwick, 47, 48
West Berlin, 33
Wilberforce, 34
William and Mary, 36
Wisconsin, 34
Yale, 36, 37
York, 47, 48, 49
University Grants Committee, 13, 26, 38, 49, 50, 103, 116, 117, 159, 160, 161, 162, 164, 166, 167, 168

vocational training, 9, 10, 29, 30, 84, 91, 96, 117, 154, 156
    see also professional training
vysshie uchebnye zavedeniya (USSR), 38–42

Wales, 10, 70, 127, 171, 181
wastage, 173, 182
    see also drop-out rates

Yugoslavia, 32

Name Index

Abbott, E., 6
Andrews, P. W. S., 175
Annan, Lord, 136
Apostdescu, N., 43
Arch, J., 5
Arnold, M., 9
Arnold, T., 16, 18, 21
Attlee, Lord, 160
Austin, M., 66–7, 69

Barker, Sir E., 165
Barnes, A. T., 5
Barnes, W. H. F., 159–69
Barrow, H., 4
Beckerman, W., 173
Beckett, J. C., 27
Bell, R. E., x, 13–28
Bellot, H., 16
Beloff, M., 151–8
Berdahl, R. O., 160
Bogomolov, A. I., 44
Boyle, R., 4
Brezinka, W., 44
Brissimis, S. N., 148–50
Brougham, 15, 16
Burgess, T., 79

Calderbank, P. H., 55–61
Campbell, L., 6
Casadevail, A. F., 129
Chain, E., 153
Chamberlain, A., 160
Charlton, H. B., 6
Cottrell, T. L., 47–54
Cox, C. B., 25
Cromwell, T., 3
Crosland, A., 116, 118

Davie, G., x, 19

Douglas, M., 71
Drever, J., 82
Dubinia, I. S., 42
Dyson, A. E., 25

Enderwitz, H., 43

Filipović, M., 32
Fromm, E., 112

Geisel, K., 43
Goldschmidt, D., 33, 44
Grant, N., 29–46

Hampson, K., 12
Hanham, H. J., 8
Hearnshaw, F. J. C., 17, 23
Hoogenboom, A., 12
Hopkinson, Sir A., 160
Hudson, L., 51, 63–73
Huxley, T. H., 9

Jacot, B., 67, 70
James, E., 43
Jefferson, T., 6, 25
Jowett, B., 6, 7, 8, 11, 22

Kath, 31, 44
Kearney, H., 1–12
Kerr, C. 175
King, E. J., 30, 43, 44
Krupin, A. V., 42, 44
Kuhlman, C., 43
Kuhn, T., 70

Lee, J., 19
Lowe, J., 115–28

Macaulay, Lord, 7–8
Mackney, A., 150

McPherson, A., 27
Manning, L., 160
Marsh, R., 93, 94
Mikhalev, G. M., 42, 44
Moody, T. W., 27
Murray, Lord, 161

Newman, J. H., 6, 16, 17
Newton, I., 4

Oehler, 31

Parris, H., 8
Pattison, A., 9
Pattison, M., 9
Picht, G., 31
Piobetta, J.-B., 32
Prokofiev, M. A., 41, 44

Reichwein, 31
Roberthall, Lord, 175
Robinsohn, S. B., 43
Rothblatt, S., 24, 27
Rutkevich, M. N., 41

Semans, H. H., 88, 89
Short, E., 128
Slepenkov, I. M., 42
Smith, Sir T., 4

Sommerkorn, I. N., 33, 44
Sparrow, J., 9
Springer, G. F., 44
Stewart, I. G., 150
Swann, M., 90, 150

Tedder, Lord, 135
Thatcher, M., 92, 109, 113
Thompson, A., 85–100
Trevelyan, Sir C., 8
Trevelyan, G. O., 7

Vaizey, J., 79, 171–83

Watson, J. Steven, 129–37
Whiting, C., 30
Whiting, C. E., 23
Wilson, T., 175
Winstanley, G., 4
Winstanley, H. M., 21, 28
Wolfe, J. N., 139–48, 151, 155, 157
Wood, Sir H., ix, 101–14
Wood, T., 2
Woodbridge, F., 8–9

Young, R., 75–84, 97, 98, 99
Youngson, A. J., 150

Zhivkov, T., 43